DO-IN

Lilian Kluivers

DO-IN

Tao-yoga for
health and energy

Following and / or applying the advice is entirely at your own risk. When in doubt, even if you experience seemingly innocent (health) problems: always consult your physician. Neither the author nor the publisher or its agents may in any way be held liable for any consequences whatsoever arising from this book.

© 2017, Wu Xing
Leiden
mail@doinacademy.com
www.doinacademy.com

Original title: Do-In, tao yoga voor gezondheid en energie
De Driehoek, Rotterdam

Design: Het vlakke land, Rotterdam
         Nina Kleingeld, Stikstof, Leiden
Photos: Lotte Stekelenburg in cooperation with Lilian Kluivers, Patrick Haak & Anushka Hofman
(clothing sponsor: www.yoga–specials.nl)
Translation: Yoff Kau

ISBN 978 90 827523 0 4
NUR 861

Contents

Part 2
Other aspects of Do-In: self-massage, breathing and meditation   119

Part 3
Do-In programs   143

Welcome!

Through this book I extend an invitation to you – in an era where most people are busy and set the bar high for themselves – to experience the body in a totally different way, namely as a trail guide to relaxation, awareness, health and energy. Do-In, a form of movement which is part of Oriental medicine, offers this possibility. According to the philosophy of Oriental medicine, the world is a unity in which everything – including human beings – is composed of energy. This energy is always in motion: day becomes night, spring turns into summer. Those who go along with that natural movement – the Tao – feel healthy, calm, relaxed and balanced. Do-In makes you aware of this natural movement and teaches you how to stimulate the self-healing flow of energy in the body.

It is my great honor to pass on this ancient knowledge, which now seems more important than ever. I hope that many people discover its beauty and efficiency and find that they become more comfortable with themselves, as I and many others experience on a daily basis.

May all beings be happy, safe, peaceful, healthy and take care of themselves happily.
(Buddhist Metta Meditation)

— Lilian Kluivers

Introduction

Stretches and breathing exercises, like you do in a yoga class or in preparation for Tai Chi, Qi Gong or other forms of movement, can help your body to remain balanced or become more balanced. Not only because these exercises stretch or relax the muscles, or because they help you to create the time needed for yourself and your breathing, but especially because the energy channels in the body, the meridians, are stretched and stimulated in the various postures.

By linking the exercises to the meridians, as Do-In does, you are able to make a powerful connection between movement and the ancient wisdom of Oriental medicine. In China and Japan, these meridian stretches, have already been practiced for over two thousand years, combined with exercises for the abdomen (which is called *hara*), breathing exercises and self-massage. In Japan this combination is called 'Do-In Ankyo' or just simply Do-In, which translates to 'flow of energy'. A clear literal translation is provided by Shizuto Masunaga, the great Japanese shiatsu therapist from the 20th century, in his book *Meridian exercises*: 'Do' (导) from Do-In means 'opening the channels and facilitating the energy flow along certain routes'. The part 'In' (引) he translates as 'stretching and moving the limbs in order to achieve this goal'. The part 'An' (按) of Ankyo means 'massaging the energy channels to balance the ki flow', and part 'Kyo' he translates into 'in a smooth motion raising the limbs'. The Do-In exercises you can perform yourself, while with Ankyo someone else performs the stretches and manipulations for you. This book covers such exercises in the duo–exercises.

Through stretching, massage and breathing exercises from Do-In new energy is awakened and balance is restored between the forces of nature, yin and yang, on which traditional Oriental therapies are based. Any obstructions will reduce or disappear, leading to new flexibility and strength.

Healing power

The idea behind these healing exercises is that if you have a healthy energy flow, you're healthy yourself and you feel calm, balanced and comfortable. Do-In is therefore a very effective way to live based upon inner strength and tranquility in the hectic everyday life of our society. But it can also be an effective preparation for meditation – that's why in some Zen monasteries it's part of the morning schedule.

Do-In exercises are a way to acquire more energy and health for all, regardless of experience or flexibility. Do-In for example, has much to offer to people who have little space to move, or even suffer from physical disabilities. The exercises for self-massage stimulate the flow of energy without taking you through complicated postures. In time joints and muscles will become more flexible and relaxed. But even for experienced athletes and yogis, the Oriental knowledge provides enrichment. With the wisdom of Do-In, is it possible to explain the healing power of yoga. How many people know that by stretching the back of your legs – for example in a standing forward bend – your Bladder and Kidney energy is strengthened? A yoga teacher said after her introduction to Do-In, 'Now I understand why I haven't suffered from cystitis since I started doing yoga! Every time I practice the Downward facing dog (a yoga posture where the back of your legs is stretched) I promote the energy flow in my Bladder-meridian!'

Eastern way of life

Do-In is derived from Taoism, the oldest philosophical system in China, and traditional Chinese medicine. The foundation of this Eastern view on life and health is not complicated, but differs from the Western view. In the West we love to make clear distinctions: this is mine, that is yours. Urban planners divide the space we have available to us into natural parks, industrial districts and living areas. Western medical science is based upon a detailed study of the body and individual organs and their functions.

Oriental medicine simply sees mind and body as an integral energetic system. Indeed, the entire universe forms an integral energetic system. And all the different planets, stars and elements within that universe are interconnected. We too are a part of this: we affect our environment and depend upon it. That is why Eastern philosophies emphasize that human beings should live in harmony with themselves and their environment in order to stay healthy. This calls for constant adaptation to changes coming from within and without. Do-In is designed to maintain or (re)find this balance.

Within the energetic complex of the universe everything consists of *ki* (also written as *Qi*, and known as *chi* in Chinese or *prana* in Indian), a Japanese word often translated as 'energy'[5]. We also consist of *ki*; our life force energy. It flows throughout the body through 'energy rivers', or meridians. There are twenty of these meridians, twelve main meridians and eight so called curious (extraordinary) meridians. Every feeling of physical or mental discomfort is seen as the result of a stagnation in the circulation of *ki*.

The names of the main meridians, for those who view them from a purely Western point of view, may sound somewhat misleading. They are named after the organs they affect. For example the Liver meridian and Kidney meridian. They flow throughout the body and not only around the organs they are named after. The Spleen meridian for instance provides energy for a number of other organs besides the spleen itself, as can be seen in Chapter 4. According to traditional Chinese medicine *ki* even precedes the formation of the body within the womb – *ki* first creates the meridians, followed by our tissues, their functions and the organs.

Do-In also takes into account that the meridians are interconnected: if one of them is blocked, then another will be lacking in energy. On the one hand this means that the cause of a complaint is not always easy to determine. A headache for example may be the result of stagnation in several meridians. But on the other hand Do-In exercises always have a positive effect on the circulation throughout the body as a whole, because a better flow in one meridian has a positive effect on all the other meridians.

The importance of prevention

Stretches, massages and breathing exercises stimulate the self healing properties of the body. Many people who practice yoga or Do-In, notice that it slowly but steadily improves their circulation, makes the joints more supple and reduces other symptoms such as menstrual complaints. They retain less water, have less pain in their back, neck and shoulders, feel comfortable and are confident. Those who practice Do-In, understand that the energy in the meridians which relates to these body parts, flows better.

The exercises therefore have a healing effect. But they were originally intended to *prevent* disease. You learn to control your energy and to stimulate the body to eliminate toxins. The idea behind this is that your fundamental energy (essence in

---

5   The character for *ki* is 氣 In Intermezzo 1 What are meridians? We elaborate on the concept of *ki*.

terms of Oriental medicine) protects you from diseases so you mature in a young and healthy body.

If this is your first introduction to Do-In, you could start with Part 3 of this book, after reading the introduction. By starting with the programs for Do-In at home, you'll start learning more from physically experiencing the practice. If you want to know more about the effect of the exercises, the way the meridians work or the backgrounds of Do-In, you can also start with the first chapters of this book. These also consist of a large number of exercises.

A brief history of Do-In

In ancient Chinese texts such as the Textbook of the Yellow Emperor (Nei Jing Su Wen), that was recorded around the fourth century BC, Do-In (Tao Yin or Dao Yin in Chinese) is referred to as a method to remain healthy. According to this text these exercises were developed in the central plains of China thousands of years ago. (That means that Do-In is probably even older than two thousand years.) At that time the inhabitants of these central plains were cultured and for most of them it was easy to feed themselves with a variety of foods. In this prosperous period people ate too much and at the same time moved less and less, which caused them to weaken. The Do-In exercises were introduced to ensure that their bodies remained balanced.

Do-In and ancient Indian yoga styles also influenced each other, as evidenced by the Japanese term 'Brahman Do-In', for specific styles. This also explains the similarities between traditional yoga postures and Do-In.

In China the Tao Yin evolved under the influence of these circumstances, Chinese medicine and Taoism. This was adopted to Do-In in Japan, where it was also influenced by Zen Buddhism. Tao Yin arose simultaneously with, or some say even earlier than, other well known arts of movement such as Tai Chi and Qi Gong.

The practice of this discipline was not without struggle. The first emperor of China, Qin Shi Huangdi, ordered all books that were not approved by his dynasty to be burned. Although not everything was burned – an ancient drawing with exercises for example was found in a tomb in Changsha in 1974 – the form of movement in that period was passed on by word of mouth. After 200 BC the exercises were once again embraced and various texts were written about them.

Although many Do-In exercises are part of martial arts, yoga and shiatsu and are practiced as such in dojos and yoga studios, the term 'Do-In' and the practice of Do-In as a powerful and complex entity passed into oblivion over the ages.[5] Besides this, the exercises were often considered as 'secret' and were transferred only from teacher to pupil. In China itself, it is said that the knowledge of Tao Yin and Qi Gong was almost forgotten at the beginning of the twentieth century.

This changed during the twentieth century. One of the reasons could be that our modern affluent society in a way was quite similar to that of the central plains of China, where Do-In was developed. We also have access to all kinds of food, and are often overeating and getting too little exercise. Do-In is kind of made for us! The first books on Do-In in the West were by Japanese shiatsu therapist and psychologist Shizuto Masunaga and the Japanese macrobiotics expert Michio Kushi. Since then, this form of movement began to be practiced more and more in both the East and the West.

Consider this

The aim of this book is to show which type of energy the different postures stimulate, circulate, regulate or calm, so you can choose the exercises that you need at any time. The meridian exercises are suitable for everyone and are great for your health – provided you have the will and perseverance to schedule some time every day for some meridian stretches, breathing techniques or massages. Are you in good health? Then feel free to combine the different exercises for the meridians yourself. Guidelines for responsible combinations of the different meridian exercises are covered in Intermezzo's 5 and 6.

As I said, this book is intended to provide guidance and insights into how readers themselves can attribute to their health in general, it's intention is not to teach you to diagnose. Diagnosing yourself or any other person is only possible after several years of study. Would you like to apply Do-In in a therapeutic way? Then I recommend that you first seek the advice of a registered shiatsu therapist, acupressure therapist, acupuncturist or any other therapist who has studied the meridians, to diagnose you. Professional associations often provide listings of registered therapists. If you like to study Do-In and become a Do-In teacher and/or private sessions, visit the website of our education Do-In Academy.

---

5   Influences of Do-In exercises are for example found in newer and interesting styles of yoga such as Okidoyoga, Meridian Yoga, Acuyoga, Yin yoga, Tsubo fitness and Zenstretching. Dao-Yin is also seen as a forerunner of Qi Gong and other energetic movement arts from China.

Though Do-In is a very safe form of movement, it is prudent to emphasize the importance of listening to your body. After reading the chapters it's most likely you'd like to perform the exercises at home, without a teacher present to help you. This means that you are responsible for reading the instructions carefully and following them to make sure that you do not inflict any injury upon yourself by forcing yourself into a posture. The exercises should feel pleasant, not painful. The body should move within its own boundaries. Only then will you reap the most benefit. Pushing or pulling yourself into a posture does not make you more flexible and will not provide you with extra energy. On the contrary, if you damage any joints, muscles or tendons you'll achieve the opposite.

Your breathing often helps to monitor your limits. Faltering breath? Then you're too deep in a stretch. To work with your body in a healthy way, it is important to always retain space to breath. This may sound obvious, but especially when you first start doing any yoga exercises, you will notice that you tend to force yourself deeper into a posture, while forgetting to breathe. Release the tension by inhaling and exhaling slowly. After you exhale it's often possible to relax even deeper.

I would also like to highlight the following general points.

Do's and don'ts of Do-In:
- Do not practice any Do-In stretches if you have a fracture, inflammation or wound; light massages *outside* the affected area may support healing.
- Do not exercise immediately after a meal.
- Do not perform stretches after surgery, let the wound heal first.
- Be especially careful in case of cancer, osteoporosis, hypertension, pregnancy, chronic fatigue syndrome, varicose veins, adhesions and scarring.
- Never perform exercises that feel uncomfortable; stay within you comfort zone. Remember that you are always responsible for your body during any form of exercise, so take that responsibility and be kind to yourself.
- For those experiencing dizziness and high blood pressure, please avoid poses with the head hanging down.
- Although Do-In promotes the healing process, it of course remains important to consult a physician in case of illness.
- Perform the exercises slowly and attentively. If you have little time, it is better that you calmly perform three to five exercises, while focusing on breathing. This is much more effective than 'quickly' doing a series of exercises.

- Infrequent practice provides only short–term results. Regular practice offers a long lasting result.
- During the exercises put aside all thoughts that are unrelated to the exercise itself and concentrate on the sensations in your body.
- Drink plenty of water or herbal tea afterwards to eliminate the toxins that were released from your body.

Contact with yourself

Before you begin with Do-In (or any form of Eastern movement), it is wise to tune in to your body by focusing on your breathing for a few minutes. For example, use the following exercise:

Sit on your knees with your buttocks on your heels (this posture is called *seiza* – in Japanese). To do *seiza* place your left foot on your right foot (or just your left big toe on the right big toe). If this posture is not comfortable, you can also sit cross-legged or sit on a chair, or stand with your feet hip-width apart, toes pointing forward, knees relaxed and turned slightly outwards, offering space for the front of the hips to open. Whatever posture you adopt, elongate to a straight back. Make space between the vertebrae, pull your chin towards your chest a little and push your crown towards the ceiling. Relax your face and shoulders and close your eyes. Relax your arms, your torso and your legs.

Focus your attention on the movement of the breath in your abdomen, feel how you inhale and feel how you exhale. If desired, lay your hands on your lower abdomen to feel the movement even better. Breathe quietly at your own pace. If a thought comes to mind, notice it, but do not get distracted: bring your attention back to your breath. If you are quickly distracted, you can count your breaths. For example you could do three series of five breaths.

Then open your eyes and begin an exercise of your choice.

Basic poses in Do-In

In order to sit in *seiza*, sit on your knees with your buttocks on your heels. Put your left foot on your right foot.

A grounded standing position begins by standing with your feet hip-width apart, toes pointing forward, knees relaxed and turned a fraction outwards, so the front of the hips opens. Visualise a three dimensional circle around you. You might also like to smile towards or 'in' your lower belly. Energy flows where attention goes.

The focus on your breath causes your center of gravity to move: out of your head, into your abdomen (the *hara*). Your mind relaxes that way, or – what often occurs – you become aware of the turmoil in your mind. This awareness that you build during breathing exercises will help you to feel the effect of a posture more accurately. As you take the time to feel the breathe and to practice exercises, your concentration will become stronger. This will make it easier for you to be less distracted by thoughts, feelings or sounds.

Breathing is the first and last thing you do in your life. Never forget that your breathing is more important and healthier than any possible exercise.

Part 1

Postures to stretch the meridians

Do-In is not difficult or complicated and does not require a lot of thinking. Therefore you do not need to memorize the information in the following chapters, before you start practicing Do-In. Memorizing will happen over time. These chapters show you what happens inside your body and how you can use the appropriate exercises to strengthen yourself. The chapters contain many exercises that help you to immediately experience what you are reading.

This first part is divided into seven chapters, each addressing two meridians that cooperate closely. Each chapter begins with two exercises, so you can immediately feel where these meridians are located. Some of these poses are known as *asanas* (postures) of yoga. Yogis who read this book, will become more aware of the healing powers of their already familiar yoga postures. Other readers will learn new exercises to explore their bodies and strengthen its self-healing properties. Visualization plays an important role in all exercises. It's not about imitating a movement, but rather visualizing the exercise while you are practicing. The power of thought stimulates the flow of energy throughout the body.

After becoming acquainted with the meridians through the exercises, there is a brief explanation about what the energy of these meridians does in your body. Even though most of the meridians carry the name of an organ, the purpose of their energy is not only limited to the operation of that organ. For example the energy also affects your mental state (if you are able to express your feelings easily, if you worry a lot, etc.) and also affects other organs. The meridian stretches in Do-In therefore have a broader effect than only the positive healing effect on the organ after which the meridian is named. And because the energy channels are interconnected, Do-In exercises indirectly strengthen the whole body.

Each chapter in Part 1 ends with even more exercises to stimulate the corresponding meridians. If for whatever reason one of the first exercises is not an option for you, then choose poses further discussed here. You can also include them to alternate with, or perform them in a series if you want to stimulate a particular meridian more intensely.

The chapters are interspersed with intermezzo's in which you can get acquainted with the theory of Oriental medicine. These intermezzos will help you to experience the exercises more deeply and understand what happens in the body during and after Do-In exercises.

The twelve basic meridians

Yin	Yang
Liver	Gallbladder
Heart	Small intestine
Heart Protector	Triple heater
Spleen	Stomach
Lung	Large Intestine
Kidney	Bladder

The meridian drawings

In all meridian drawings (see pages 20, 34, etc.) the acu-points are numbered in the order in which they appear on the meridian. A meridian either runs from a finger or toe into the body, or from a location on the body towards a finger or toe: the direction is based upon the fact whether it is a yin- or a yang-meridian. The first point on the meridian, for example that of the Lung, is – besides it's Chinese or Japanese name – mostly just called Lung 1 (Lu1) and this is how the numbers progress.

The more people that work on their inner balance, the closer we get to world peace.

1 Communication, mental flexibility, breathing and letting go

Do-In for Lung and Large intestine

Getting acquainted with the meridians

This chapter shows you where the energy pathways of the Lung and Large intestine are located, what their function is and how you can strengthen them. The chapter begins with two exercises that stimulate these meridians so you can experience the energy channels immediately.

Stretch for Lung energy

Stand with your feet slightly wider than shoulder distance apart, your toes pointing slightly outward. Place your hands with the fingers interlaced on the back of your head. Rotate your shoulders down and back. Move your elbows back and open your chest, look up slightly. Then turn to the left as far as you can. Lift your right heel and twist even a little further. Your left foot remains flat on the ground. Push your left elbow up and back so you feel your armpit being stretched open. Gaze beyond your left elbow into the distance. Slowly breathe in and out, three to five times. Then turn back to the front. Perform the stretch twisting to the other side and repeat 5 times on both sides. In this exercise, you will feel a stretch across your chest muscles and your upper arm, exactly along the pathway of the Lung meridian.

The Lung meridian (=Lu) originates in a indentation next to your shoulder, an inch below the collarbone. It runs over the shoulder, through the biceps along the front side of the arm towards the crease of the elbow. And from there it runs along the forearm to the medial corner of the thumbnail. Internally the meridian runs from the diaphragm along the large intestine to about waist height, then back up through the stomach and into the lungs.

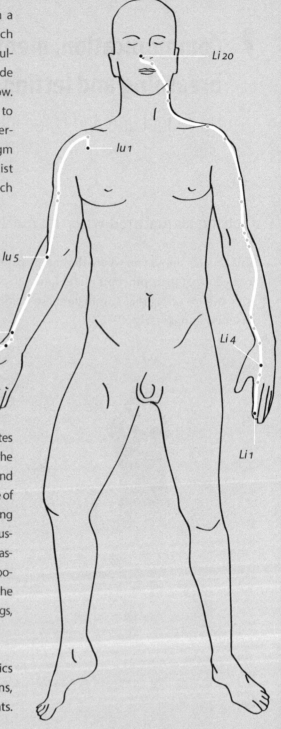

Li 20

lu 1

lu 5

lu 7
lu 9

Li 4

lu 11

Li 1

The Large intestine meridian (= LI) originates next to cuticle of the nail on the thumb side of the index finger. It runs along the index finger and the forearm towards the outside of the crease of the elbow. From there, the meridian runs along the outer arm, over the shoulder along the muscle on the side of your neck (m. sternocleidomastoideus). It ends next to the nostril on the opposite side of where the meridian began. From the shoulder an internal branch runs along the lungs, and through the large intestine.

P.S. for an explanation of the characteristics of the described acu-points on the meridians, check page 168: appendix acupressure points.

Stretch for Large intestine energy

Sit cross-legged. Place your right hand next to you on the floor. Then bend your left ear toward your left shoulder. You now feel a stretch on the side of your neck. Straighten your neck after three slow breaths and change sides. Repeat three times. In this position you feel the Large intestine meridian stretching along the side of your neck.

Lung and Large intestine: partners

Lungs take the purest element of our outside world: air; or, in terms of Oriental medicine, the *ki* – life force – of the universe. The Large intestine, on the other hand, rids the body of everything that is no longer needed. Oriental medicine, in addition to the purely physical and local operation of organs, takes a broader, holistic way of looking at things. It subdivides the organs into duos – also called element or transformation – because of their shared mental and spiritual role.

Lung and Large intestine form such a duo. Together, these organs symbolize the exchange with our environment, including communication. When the energy of the Lungs and Large intestine is strong, you are able to have discussions without feeling that your opinions are inferior or more important than those of other people. In addition, you feel connected to the rest of the world.

Breathing is therefore our most direct connection with life. Before birth our mother provides the functions of lung and large intestine: the baby receives oxygen through the umbilical cord and through the same connection eliminates waste products. The first thing a baby does after its birth is breathe. It is an exchange between you as an individual and the outside world.

But how does the intake of *ki* from the universe work? The Lungs suck in the *ki* energy and send it down to the Kidneys. Only then, does this energy, according to the Oriental point of view, spread throughout the rest of the body. This means that through shallow breathing, you will benefit less from it. If you're breathing the wrong way for a prolonged period of time, you could even start feeling chronically fatigued. That's why abdominal breathing is very important.

Also the large intestine will benefit from calm, deep breathing: with each inhalation, the intestines are slightly compressed by the expanding lungs and as a result the abdomen moves forward. With each exhalation the lungs empty themselves, which makes more room for the intestines in the lower abdomen. The movement of the breath is like a massage for the intestines. This promotes the natural contracting movement of the intestines (peristalsis), which aids digestion and enhances the flow in our bellies. At the same time deep breathing helps to prevent or alleviate problems such as irritable bowel syndrome and constipation.

Beyond grief

All meridians also influence our emotional well being. Confidence and a sense of justice are the positive emotions that belong to the Lung energy. Not being able to deal with grief, such as not being able to express or let go of sadness, shows that the Lung energy is imbalanced.

Everyone is touched with sadness at some point in their life, this is inevitable. But people with a healthy Lung energy can deal with the changes that are caused by grief, accept their loss, refind treir strengh and open themselves again to new impressions after a period of mourning. Do-In exercises for the Lungs and Large intestine assist in letting go of old emotions and habits.

Visualization for letting go

Stand with your feet hip-width apart, with your toes and knees facing forward. Let your arms hang at your sides so that your palms face backwards. Now move your arms forwards and backwards. Bend and straighten your knees to the rhythm of your swing. Imagine that you let go every time you swing your hands back. You could imagine anything here: work, stress, thoughts, sadness. Choose whatever applies to your situation.

What does the Lung energy do?

The Lung energy supports the lung function. For example it provides the lungs with the energy they need to take in oxygen and release carbon dioxide.

But the Lung meridian does more than that. As mentioned before, the energy from the air, according to Chinese medicine needs to connect to the Kidneys. This is done through the Lung- and Kidney meridian. But for this connection to occur, the breath has to be deep enough to move the abdomen forward. Only then can we most effectively use energy from the air. This energy is distributed throughout the body during the exhalation. The ancient Oriental healers, who derived their wisdom purely from observation and touch – and not through performing operations– described the events during the expiration as follows: during the exhalation mist rises from the Kidneys. The Lung meridian then diffuses this mist to the surface, right up underneath the skin. This mist provides elasticity to the skin and gives it a healthy sheen.

The Lungs also influence our defensive *ki* that circulates between the skin and muscles. This supports the immune system, particularly in the skin, nose and throat.

The Lungs are also connected to the skin and our nervous system. They control the rhythm of our lives (think of the rhythm of our breathing), allowing the *ki* to descend and disperse into our body.

Nourishment for the Lung

If you recently caught a cold, for example during a bike ride through the rain, food with a sharp taste can help the protective energy of the Lung meridian in a sense to sweat out the cold. For example, create a spicy soup with leeks, onion, garlic, pepper and ginger. The sharp taste opens the pores, spreads the energy quickly and awakens the senses. Mucus dissolves, so you might get a runny nose.

However, if there is a deficiency of *ki* due to a chronically decreased lung function (eg. severe chronic lung diseases), the effect of the sharp taste (the temporary energy distribution and the opening of the pores) might further decrease the energy. In that case it is more beneficial to opt for mildly-spicy dishes such as a potato-leek soup.

Becoming ill

According to Oriental medicine there are five harmful external influences that can make us ill: cold, moisture, wind, heat and dryness. Spending prolonged time in any of these circumstances, can throw our energy for a loop, and thus the body, off balance. Let's stick to the example of the bicycle ride in the rain (see the box about Nourishment for the Lungs). The adverse external influences like moisture and cold can enter the body and make us catch a cold. You can protect yourself against such external influences, through clothing, climate of a room (air conditioning or heating on a low setting, so the contrast with outside is not too big) and through food as shown in the example in the box about nourishment for the Lungs.

Besides these external pathogenic factors, other examples that can cause illnesses are chronic stress and negative emotions, like anxiety, worry, fear, grief and anger.

What do you notice when the Lung meridian is out of balance?

Because Oriental medicine operates from a holistic view of the body, it is impossible to provide a list of complaints that are guaranteed to occur when there's a problem with the Lung energy, because all things interact in relation to each other. For example the Lung meridian is always involved in respiratory issues such as shallow breathing. But this does not mean that the Lung energy is always to be recognized as the weakest link. An imbalance in the Spleen or Liver could also be a cause of Lung dysfunction. Check to see in which meridians you recognize the most symptoms for your specific case, and focus on exercises and especially self-massages for these energy pathways.

Another common example would be headaches. A headache is not always due to the same cause and therefore does not always ask for the same treatment. Some complaints are therefore listed with multiple organs. In this case, try to identify which meridian you associate the majority of the symptoms with and during Do-In focus on stimulating the flow of that meridian. Intermezzo 5: *The cycle of life: the Five transformations* also provides instructions on how you can use Do-In to strengthen the energy in the meridians.

The following list gives you an idea of symptoms that may occur when there are problems with the energy of the Lungs.

Physical:
- Itchy nose
- Sneezing
- Susceptible to colds and coughs

- Throat complaints
- Hoarseness
- Asthma
- Shortness of breath, labored breathing
- Bronchitis
- Scratchy or piercing voice
- Fluid retention in upper body (edema)
- Dry skin (including eczema and psoriasis)
- Constipation
- Colitis
- Body odor that smells of decay (the smell of overripe cabbage)
- Watery eyes
- Pasty color on the face, or white skin around the eyes

Mental:
- Prevalent feeling of melancholy or depression
- Inability to mourn
- Feelings of isolation
- Inability to enter into relationships
- Dominant and possessive behavior
- Excessive worrying combined with shortness of breath

What does the Large intestine energy do?

Part of the energy pathway of the Large intestine reaches the large intestine by means of a deep branch of the meridian. This energy supports the large intestine in absorbing water, nutrients and vitamin K. Indigestible food travels through to the last section of the digestive tract, the rectum, to be eliminated from the body. This energy also helps you to rid yourself of waste through your skin, think of pimples and rashes for example. The large intestine is therefore a symbol of excretion – not only of digestion. Mentally, for example, you can release stress through a breathing exercise where you deliberately prolong the exhalation, symbolic of spending more time on letting go (exhaling) than taking in (inhaling). This 'letting go' is an activity connected to the Large intestine meridian. Also, this energy helps you to let go of old patterns of behavior. If specific behavior once helped you to belong to a certain group of people, this could stand in your way later on in life because you do not really feel like yourself. Releasing this behavior, is an act of the Large intestine energy.

What do you notice if the Large intestine energy is out of balance?
The following symptoms are common to an imbalance of the Large intestine energy. Exercises that stimulate the circulation in the meridian are beneficial in such cases.

Physical:
- Diarrhea or on the other side of the spectrum constipation
- Lower back pain (lumbar)
- Cold abdomen
- Poor circulation in the legs
- Flatulence
- Hay fever
- Cold
- Rash
- Lack of facial expression
- Shoulder pain and tennis elbow
- Pain in the neck that radiates to the arm and (sometimes) index finger
- Stuffy nose
- Nosebleeds
- Sinusitis
- Toothache
- Hemorrhoids
- Bloodshot eyes
- Tendency to be inert

Mental:
- Unable to let go
- Inability to express emotions
- Lack of friends
- Insignificant energy to develop yourself
- Quickly losing motivation

Exercises to balance the Lung and Large intestine energy

The following exercises will improve the circulation of Lung and Large intestine energy. With this selection of exercises you will learn to recognize the pathway of these two meridians. Other exercises that stretch the same areas, also strengthen these meridians.

Stretching the Lungs

Sit down on your knees in the posture that is called *seiza*, or any other sitting posture if *seiza* is not possible. Lift your right arm diagonally, just above shoulder height; the thumb is pointing upwards and slightly back. Rotate your right arm further back until you feel a pleasant stretch on the inside of your arm. Change sides after five to ten breaths.

Effect: In this exercise you are stretching the Lung meridian, and this opens up your lungs and gives more space to breathe. Because it relaxes the muscles in your chest, this exercise can also assist in more easily keeping your upper back straight, because it releases tension from the upper back.

Stretching the forearms

Position yourself on your hands and knees. Your hands are directly below your shoulders, knees below your hips. Now reverse the position of your hands carefully. The back of your hands is now on the floor now, instead of the palm of your hands. Point the fingers towards your knees. You now feel a stretch on the front of your arms, along Large intestine meridian (as well as the Small intestine and Triple heater meridians which you will see in the next chapters).

Be careful during this exercise, because the wrists and lower arms can be pretty stiff.
Are they very flexible? Then you could lean backwards a bit in this position to intensify the stretch. Remind yourself to respect the boundaries of your body.

After five breaths, move back to a neutral position and place the palms of your hands on the floor again.

Lift your hands and shake your wrists loosely as if you want to shake off drops of water until the wrists feel completely relaxed.

Move back onto your hands and knees again. Now position your hands so that the thumbs point to the sides (outward) and the fingers back towards your knees, or as far as you can get if pointing to the knees is not possible. The palms of your hands now remain on the floor. Move out of this position after five breaths and shake your wrists softly.

Effect: In this posture you stretch the inside of your lower arms, the Lung meridian (as well as the meridian of the Heart and Heart protector as you will see in the following chapters). Be careful, because this side of the lower arms can also be very stiff.

Stretching the lungs and large intestine while bending forward

Take a wide straddle pose standing with your toes slightly turned out. Hook your thumbs together behind your back. Look up while you inhale, pull your shoulder blades toward each other and open your lungs. Exhale and bend from the hips. Stretch your arms away from your back and pull your shoulder blades together and down towards your hips. Come back to upright position after five to ten breaths. Take a moment to feel the relaxation in your arms, back and chest. Hook your other thumb, then perform the exercise again.

Effect: This exercise opens the lungs, and stretches a branch of the Large intestine meridian on the outer side of the back of the legs. Sometimes the shoulders get stiff which makes it impossible to lift the arms away from the back. This is not important. Perform the exercise to your ability. If you feel a pleasant stretch and continue breathing calmly and deeply, then you're doing well. Don't worry, your flexibility will improve over time.

Note: in case of hypertension is not recommended to hang your head lower than hip-level. Instead you should choose to perform this exercise without bending over.

Yawning

Yawning causes more oxygen to enter your blood. Rub both hands over your face near your mouth and nose (where the Large intestine meridian runs). Then stretch your arms outward and open your mouth. Look upwards upon inhalation with your arms raised and stretched back, so you open the Lung meridian. Try to yawn. Exhale while lowering your arms.

Mudra

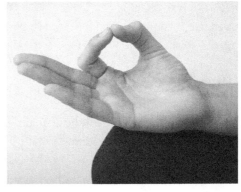

Sit cross-legged, or in any other pleasant sitting posture. Place your hands upon your knees with the palms facing up. Place the tip of your thumb against the tip of your index finger. This connects the energy of lung and large intestine, the exercise is also known as *jnana-* or *chin mudra*. Take at least five minutes to observe your breath in this position. Breathe slowly and deeply, let your abdomen move along with the breath. To enhance the energy-flow you could also place your thumb at the cuticle of the index finger (medial side), on the acupressure point LI 1.

Effect: This *mudra* (a symbolic posture) encourages taking in what you need and releases what you no longer need. You may also notice that it becomes easier to breathe into your abdomen as you perform this *mudra*. Mentally this *mudra* pulls you into the 'now', because when the energy circulation of the Large intestine is enhanced, you become less preoccupied with thoughts. This clears the mind. If you want, you could visualize which things you want to take in (for example new energy) and which things you'd like to let go of.

> ## Feeling
>
> While practicing Do-In exercises there is a lot to take notice of. Does it feel smooth? Slow? Fast? Deep? Can you relax just that extra bit? Can you manage to remain calm and breathe deeply? Try not to let your thoughts carry you away during Do-In but perform the exercises while being very aware of what is happening right here, right now. Feel the difference before and after an exercise, between the left and the right side of your body and also between the side you've already stretched and the side you haven't stretched yet. Practice Do-In as if it were a meditation in motion.

Intermezzo 1
What are meridians?

Rivers of energy

In this intermezzo you will be acquainted with the fundaments of Chinese medicine; you will read about meridians, what the meaning of *ki* is and why it is important to keep this *ki* strong.

The Oriental view on the body is based upon a system of meridians, energy channels, through which the life force energy, *ki*, flows. These meridians are comparable to rivers or arteries, but just as the *ki*, they are not tangible or visible – and can usually only be felt by people who have been properly trained. When the *ki* flows uninterrupted through the meridians, then our body – which is an expression of our *ki* – is healthy: the life force energy reaches each cell. However it is also possible that the *ki* in the meridians becomes stagnant, or even may flow in the wrong direction, for example due to the influence of extreme cold, heat, drought, stress, emotions or germs. A meridian that is unable to properly flow, could be envisioned as a river that has a dam built in it: the area before the dam overflows, the area behind the dam is not being provided with anything. When there is a stagnation like that in one of our energy channels, we experience complaints. At the beginning the symptoms are inconspicuous: tension, fatigue, skin rash or nagging pain. When the stagnation persists, the complaints will become more intense over time.

Organs and meridians
According to the Chinese and Japanese point of view the body is comparable to an empire wherein each organ performs its own role. For example the heart is recognized as the emperor, and most of the others organs could be seen as ministers that are performing the task of transforming or distributing nutrients or ingredients throughout the body.

To ensure the harmony within the body, the organs have to communicate with each other. They do this through the system of meridians. Each meridian flows throughout the body on a deeper level through one or more organs, but also directly under the skin. This is why it is possible to see from someone's appearance what is going on internally and it is possible to use external treatments and physical exercises to influence the more deep seated energy system. Physically, as Steven Birch and Kiiko Matsumoto clearly point out in their book *Hara Diagnosis, Reflections on the Sea*, the meridians are nowadays recognised as the fascia that conduct the energy through our body.

The ancient meridian system consists of twelve primary meridians and eight extraordinary vessels. These are also all connected to each other through side-branches. They begin and end at specific locations in the body and the energy flows up (yin) or down (yang) through them. The twelve primary meridians are named after the organ that they are most connected to. The other eight vessels run deeper in the body and can be seen as storage warehouses of *ki*.

What is *ki*?

The words *ki*, *Qi* and *chi* are prevalent in the Japanese and Chinese language, often as part of another word. But in English there is not one other word to be found that completely covers the true meaning of *ki*.

To avoid misconception most writers chose to not translate this word and simply leave it as it is. When it is translated the most common words used are energy, breath, life force energy, inspiration, harmony, primal matter, vitality, force or ether.

Rice and steam
Still it is important, if we are to understand the Oriental view of the body, to have an idea to go with this word. From the different suggested translation as given above, it is evident that *ki* is an untouchable and yet all pervasive form of energy that truly is omnipresent. The character for *ki* (氣) is built out of two parts. The upper portion stands for steam, gas, vapor. The lower part stands for uncooked rice. This character reveals a lot about the nature of *ki*: it shows that *ki* can both manifest itself as immaterial as seen in vapor, but at the same time as solid as rice. It also shows that *ki* is a very subtle substance (gas, vapor) that can arise from a solid substance, such as steam arises when rice is being cooked. Furthermore the symbol for rice – the primary source of nutrition in China and Japan – shows us that as part of the symbol for *ki* that *ki* also nourishes the body. The 'gas' component is seen as a symbol of the dynamic nature of consciousness. Viewed from that perspective the symbol for *ki* would loosely translate to: body and mind.

The Taoist master Mantak Chia poignantly describes it in his book *Tao Yin* as: "An ever changing, forever flowing force, an energy that can appear and disappear, can be strong and weak, can be controlled but can also be overwhelming."

In summary: *ki* is not material, but material things are made up of *ki*, in this respect rocks and bones are a very crude form of *ki*. Contrary to that the *ki* in meridians and the air is very refined. And because *ki* in coarse or refined form can adapt into an infinite number of shapes, it is so extremely difficult to translate. It actually is everything.

The origin of the body according to Oriental healing
According to Oriental healing, even before there is any suggestion of the development of tissue, initially there is *ki*: the potential energy from which the body later can be formed. Out of this *ki* meridians develop. These enable the supply of energy, so that tissues can start to develop, followed by organs. When a baby develops in the belly, according to this perspective, the meridians – especially the extraordinary vessels – are present first and the new body forms itself around them.

Translated to a mature body in the case of the liver this means that it is only present because of liver *ki*. When the liver *ki* is stagnated for a prolonged period, this also has consequences for the organ itself.

Often people ask what happens to a meridian if an organ, for example a kidney, is removed: does the Kidney meridian then also disappear?

Fortunately you cannot cut out meridians. They will find a new pathway if the tissue that they were connected to, is removed. The meridian in this case often will be more susceptible to imbalance, making it all the more important to maintain it well for example through Do-In and a healthy life-style.

2 Digestion
Do-In for Spleen and Stomach

Getting acquainted with the meridians

This chapter shows you where the energy pathways of the Spleen and Stomach are located, what their function is and how you can strengthen them. The chapter begins with two exercises that stimulate these meridians so that you can experience the energy channels immediately.

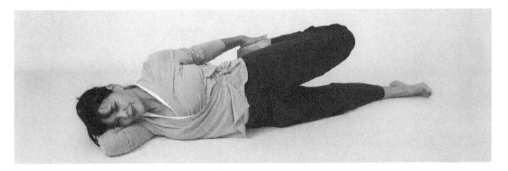

Stretch 1 for the energy of Stomach and Spleen

Lie down on your right side and support your head with your right hand. Bend your left leg, hold your left knee slightly apart from your right knee. Grab the left foot with your left hand. If you cannot reach your foot, you could wrap a shawl or belt around your foot. Now pull your foot towards your left buttock and push your hips forward. You will feel a stretch along the front of your upper leg. Hold this position for five to ten relaxed breaths, then release the position and change sides and repeat. Experience the improved flow throughout your leg after the exercise. In this posture you stretch two meridians: those of both the Stomach and the Spleen. Because these are located quite close to one and other you almost always stretch them simultaneously. Be aware that if you have problems with the knees it might be easier to perform this exercise while lying belly down on the floor.

The **Spleen meridian (=sp)** originates next to the cuticle on the medial side of the large toe. The meridian continues along the inside of the foot and ankle, along the edge of the shin, the knee and the thigh upwards. From the groin the meridian runs over the lower abdomen up along the chest and then bends back down the side of the rib cage. Internally the Spleen meridian runs along the heart, stomach, spleen, pancreas and tongue. Apart from this the meridian also connects to the ovaries.

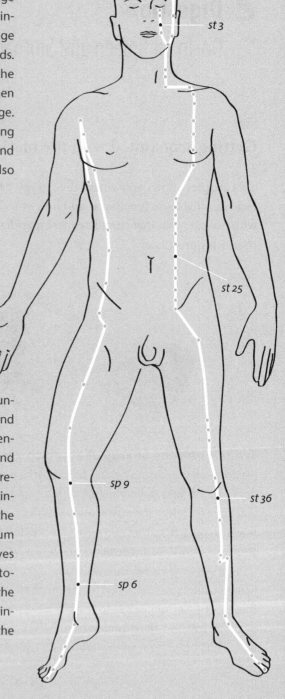

The **Stomach meridian** begins straight under the pupil on the orbit (eye socket) and runs down along the mouth. There the energy channel connects with the gums and has a small branch along the jaw to the forehead. From the mouth the meridian continues along the throat, the clavicle, over the chest and nipple. Right under the sternum (breastbone) the meridian slightly curves and runs along the abdominal muscles towards the pubic bone and further down the thigh, the knee and the outside of the shinbone towards the second toe. Internally the meridian connects to the stomach.

Stretch 2 for the energy of Stomach and Spleen

Lie down on your back. Place your feet behind your hips on the floor. Align the toes straight forward and keep the feet at hip distance. Place your arms along the body with the palms facing the floor. Lift your hips up from the floor as high as you can on an inhalation and create a straight line from your knees to your shoulders. Keep your feet on the floor and push your knees away from you. Lower your hips on the next exhalation while lowering yourself vertebra by vertebra. Repeat five to ten times and the last time keep your hips elevated for at least five breaths. During this exercise you are resting on your shoulders and not on your neck. If you have neck problems, be extra careful while lifting the hips. This exercise is beneficial for both the Stomach as well as the Spleen energy.

Spleen and Stomach: partners

The pancreas actually also belongs to this duo. It is governed by the Spleen meridian. The meridians of these organs combined take care of the first phase of the digestive tract and the absorption of nutrients. The Spleen meridian plays a role together with all the organs that excrete digestive enzymes, such as the stomach, the intestines and the pancreas, which produces enzymes that assist in digesting proteins and fats. Apart from that the pancreas supplies insulin to regulate the blood sugar level.

Besides their combined capacity in the digestion, the broader holistic assignment of these meridians is associated with grounding, receiving, giving, stability, nutrition, fertility – not purely physical, but also mentally by having new ideas – and support.

Acceptance

The spiritual function of these organs is to assist us in accepting as well as to ground us. Those who do not accept the changing realities, find themselves fretting and brooding and becoming trapped in thought.

Fretting and brooding – a symptom of imbalance in the energy of the Stomach and Spleen – depletes the energy of these organs further. An extreme example is a person with an intellectual job, who also takes twenty books with him on holiday. This insatiable lust for knowledge is a symptom of an overactive Stomach and Spleen meridian, which eventually will have consequences for the health of the organs.

The emotion connected to the stomach and spleen, is empathy. Someone with a healthy balance within this pair of meridians will recognize when another person needs a listening ear and shows understanding at exactly the right moments. This can easily go overboard due to imbalance, so that someone feels the need to care for everyone, with an unintentional motive being the desire to feel accepted themselves. On the other end of the spectrum, an inability to empathize with others is equally prevalent.

Sweet

When the energy channels of stomach and spleen become imbalanced, the body is less effective at absorbing nutrition. This makes us crave sweets, because sweet products give us fast and plentiful energy. But refined sugars (the sugars in mostly all snacks) just deepen the imbalance. Because these sugars are released into your bloodstream so rapidly, the pancreas (which is governed by the Spleen meridian) has to work very hard to regulate the blood sugar level. Resulting in this organ yearning for energy, which again makes you crave sweets.

Revert to light products then? Unfortunately, this is also not the solution. When we taste the (artificial) sweet taste, the pancreas – which cannot distinguish between the sweet taste of sugar and that of synthetic sweeteners – already sends the hormone insulin into the blood, so the expected sugars can be assimilated into energy. Because insulin doesn't work with fake sugar, the insulin level in the blood rises. And that then needs to be balanced by initiation of a sense of hunger and mostly a craving for sugar.

So instead of choosing candy or pastry, try dried apricots for example. Also grains and vegetables like carrots, which have a naturally sweet taste, do indeed help to strengthen the meridians of the Stomach and Spleen. Besides that these natural sugars have a soothing and calming effect.

What does the energy of the Spleen do?

The spleen can be seen as a type of filter that filters pathogens (germs) and aged blood cells out of our blood and digests them, after which the liver processes the remains further. We can indeed continue living without a spleen. This does however have consequences: without a spleen for example your physical resistance will be weaker.

Of course the Spleen energy has more tasks: it is responsible for the conversion of food into usable components for the body and the distribution of these throughout our body. The energy channel also provides for the functioning of the pancreas. Besides that the Spleen energy also makes it possible for everything in the body to remain in its rightful place: prolapse of organs as well as varicose veins develop from a weakened Spleen energy. The spleen also has a task concerning mental processes: with a strong Spleen energy you are able to concentrate and focus well.

What do you experience when the Spleen energy is imbalanced?
When the Spleen is imbalanced, you might recognize this from the following symptoms:

Physical:
- Lack of appetite
- Or instead continual hunger and craving
- Fatigue after eating
- Fatigued muscles
- Watery excrement and undigested food particles
- Constipation combined with a sedentary life and brainwork
- Loose and flabby flesh
- Or instead lumpy fat or bunched up flesh
- Blood in saliva, stools or urine
- Nose bleeds
- Broken capillaries, varicose veins
- Prolonged or abundant menstruation
- Alternative menstrual complaints
- Miscarriages
- Fluid under the skin, edema
- Large amounts of vaginal discharge
- Prolapse (organs, facial skin, breasts)
- PMS combined with fatigue and painful breasts

- Frozen shoulder
- Front of the legs easily becomes chilly

Mental:
- Mental fatigue
- ADHD
- A sense that everything is too much, being overwhelmed
- A need to thoroughly analyze and understand everything
- Worrying
- Involving yourself with (the work of) others
- Caring for others in search of appreciation for yourself

What does the Stomach energy do?

A strong Stomach energy is extremely important to achieve a sense of vitality. After the mouth the stomach is the organ in the chain of digestion where transformation of food into usable building materials occurs. If the stomach is not able to perform its task, this will lead to weakening and loss of energy. When the Stomach is weak, this leads to the other organs weakening as a result of a deficiency of *ki*, life force energy.

What do you experience when the Stomach energy is imbalanced?
When the energy of the Stomach declines, which could happen for example by eating too many cold meals, worrying or excessive stress, this could lead to several types of upset stomach. But because the Stomach meridian is connected through a deep branch with the mouth and the gums, problems could also arise here. Many of these complaints are connected to age, because the Stomach energy weakens as we grow older. This is a natural process. This weaker Stomach energy also presents itself through pale and narrow lips, which we often see in older people. Pink full lips are seen as a sign of youthfulness and energy (that is one of the reasons why woman have their lips 'injected' or use lipstick; which offers them the illusion of looking younger and healthier than they actually are).

Other symptoms that are indicative of an imbalance in the Stomach meridian, are:

Physical:
- Bleeding gums, canker sores or ulcers
- Inability to taste

- Thin or pale (upper) lips
- Dry, white withdrawing gums
- Bad breath
- Excessive appetite
- Stomach pain
- Dry mouth
- Morning fatigue
- Bloated feeling
- Belching
- Hiccups
- Vomiting
- Nausea
- Cold sore on the mouth
- Painful at the corners of the mouth
- Sour taste in mouth

Mental:
- Destructive neuroses
- Anorexia and bulimia
- Turning down compliments
- The tendency to only give and care for others
- Fretting and worrying
- Useless feelings of regret
- Emotion eating

Exercises for balancing Spleen and Stomach energy

To strengthen your digestion, you can do all kinds of exercises that stretch the front of your body, in addition to eating healthy food. The following exercises are very effective because they stretch the Stomach and Spleen meridian and through doing that enhance this energy flow. Also the self-massages as described in Part 2 are very effective in case of weakness or blockages.

Balance

Start standing up straight with both feet on the ground. Move your weight into one leg, and pull up your other foot to your buttock. Grab that foot with your hand. Keep your knees together, push your hip forward and your tailbone down to relieve pressure in your lower back. Keep your upper body stretched upright. To stay balanced it helps to focus your eyes on one spot, but you can also lean your hand on something or even place it against an imaginary wall. Effect: In this posture you stretch the meridians of the Stomach and Spleen; this relaxes the muscles in the upper legs, which enhances the circulation.

Stomach massage

Seat yourself on your knees in *seiza*, or in cross-legged position. Curl the tips of your fingers under your ribs and bend forward on an exhalation. Your ribs now slide over your fingers. On the inhalation your straighten up again. Maybe you can even experience the flow of fresh blood to your internal organs, which are situated right under your ribs.
Effect: This exercise relaxes the diaphragm. Repeat five times.

Stretch laying down for Stomach and Spleen

The first steps of this exercise are possible for most people, but the ultimate posture is an exercise for the advanced practitioner.

Start once again on your knees in *seiza*. Sit on your heels or between your feet. Slowly lean back and walk your hands backwards. Find your boundary: either lean on your hands or elbows, or lie down fully on your shoulders. Push your hips forward and tailbone towards the knees to keep the lower back as relaxed as possible. Press your lower legs into the floor. Once you are fully down on your shoulders, you can bring the hands up over your head. Place the hands

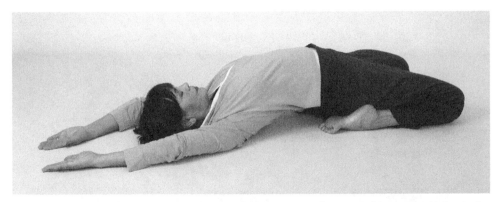

palms up and stretch out. Keep the knees together as much as possible to stretch both the Stomach and Spleen meridians.

This exercise is very difficult if you have stiff knees or ankles. You can make the exercise less difficult by placing a pillow or a folded duvet or blanket under your back.

Effect: The exercise strengthens the energy of Stomach and spleen, relaxes the muscles on the front of the legs and improves the circulation in the legs.

Intense stretch

The next exercise is very demanding and especially good for people that hardly felt a stretch in the upper legs during the previous Do-In exercise.

Start out on your knees and bring your right foot to the floor. Place your right hand on your right knee and lean forward as far as possible with your hips facing forward. You can already feel the Spleen meridian opening in your groin. Drop the left hip towards the ground. Ideally your legs will form a straight line between your knees. You can place a pillow under the bottom knee if you need one. This position will already give you a stretch in the front of your hip.

If you want to intensify, you can grab your left foot with your left hand and pull it towards your hips to stretch both the stomach and the Spleen meridian in your upper leg. Breathe towards the tension. After five to ten breaths you can switch sides.

Locust

Lay down on your belly with your fists pressed into the soft part of your groin. Place your forehead or chin on the ground. Bring the feet together and lift your legs up on an inhale. Remain with your legs raised for five to ten breaths. Stretch a little more and then release the legs on an exhale. Remove the hands out from under the groin and relax.

Effect: During this exercise your fists give pressure into the groin along the Stomach and Spleen meridian. This enhances blood circulation in the hip area and stimulates purification of the blood.

Be aware: with low back problems you should perform this exercise without lifting the feet off the floor. Because we lie on our belly in this position, it is not suited for pregnancy after the first trimester. In cases of osteoarthritis the fists in the groin can feel painful. The alternative is leaving the hands beside you.

Intermezzo 2
Yin and yang

The foundation for balance

In this intermezzo you will read about the philosophical concepts of yin and yang and how these manifest as energy in the body, as well as how you can stimulate the balance between yin and yang through Do-In.

The foundation of the Eastern philosophy is the model of yin and yang. This model was conceived more than 4000 years ago to explain the complexity of reality in a simple fashion.

The idea is simple. Yin and yang represent qualities that are in opposition to each other and at the same time complement each other. The image also represents this: it is a circle, symbolizing unity, which consists of two parts. The white half of the circle represents the sunny side of the mountain for yang, where all is visible. The black half represents the shadow side, which is hidden from the sun. This already offers the first contradiction as well as supplement: light and dark, or warm and cold. The symbol shows this through the white dot in the dark half and the dark dot in the white half: day always becomes night and therefore holds within itself a seed of the night. Night always becomes day again. In that sense yin can always transform into yang and vice versa. This is also symbolized by the wave motion of the line through the middle: much yang and less yin (daytime) automatically transforms into less yang and more yin (the night). The exchange from day into night, warmth into cold and seasons are seen as the collaboration between yin and yang. It is our task to continually adjust ourselves to the interaction between the forces of heaven and earth, and thus to become and feel part of the whole.

Everything is relative
Because everything to a certain degree is yin and yang, you can only speak of yin and yang in a relative sense. 'Earth is yin' therefore is a strange expression. It depends on

what you are comparing it with. Earth for example is yin as compared to the warm sun. But yang as compared to the naturally cool and fluid water.

Yin and yang within the body

The body can also be seen as a balance between yin and yang. Eastern healing – and therefore also Do-In – have the ultimate goal of restoring a possible imbalance between these two forces within the body. This imbalance as it happens is probably the primary reason for diseases.

If we were to walk on all fours as animals do, then the spots that have the sun shining on them are yang. This would be our backs, outside of the arms, top and back of the head, back and outsides of the legs. Yang in this sense represents heavenly energy.

The spots that are not touched by the warmth of the sun when we are in this position are more yin – the face, inside of arms, abdomen, inside and front of the legs. Yin is the earthly energy. Man is also seen as 'a child of heaven and earth', existing of energy streams of yang and yin.

But the division between yin and yang in our body goes further: meridians are also subdivided into yin and yang. The yin meridians are: Liver, Heart, Heart protector, Spleen, Lung and Kidney. These meridians and their associated organs are responsible for transformation, circulation and storage of *ki* and blood. The yang meridians are: Gallbladder, Small intestine, Triple heater, Stomach, Large intestine and Bladder. The organs that belong to this set are hollow organs in our digestive tract. They are occupied with absorbing and processing food and eliminating waste products. In the body, sets of yin and yang meridians are always closely collaborating, such as the Liver and the Gallbladder and the Heart and Small intestine. In these pairs the yin organ (Liver and Heart) is always seen as the most important. The yang meridian is sort of the sidekick and assists the yin meridian.

Yin-meridian	Yang-meridian
Liver	Gallbladder
Heart	Small intestine
Heart protector	Triple heater
Spleen	Stomach
Lung	Large intestine
Kidney	Bladder

Yin side and yang side

It's not that miraculous that almost all yang meridians run along the yang side of our body. All yin meridians run along the yin side of our body.

Just as rivers that have water running through them, the *ki* in the meridians has a specific direction it flows in.

The yin meridians flow from the bottom to the top (from earth to heaven) and the yang meridians flow from top to bottom (from heaven to earth). To bring the above theory more to life, I've listed a number of examples from daily life below, which are relative in yin and yang to each other.

Ying and Yang qualities

Yin	Yang
Form	Energy
Earth	Heaven
Peace	Activity
Stillness	Movement
Nourishing	Protecting
Cooling	Warming
Dark	Light
Moon	Sun
New Moon	Full Moon
Space	Time
Right	Left
Material	Immaterial
Under	Above
Water	Fire
Inside	Outside
Front	Back
Feminine	Masculine

Yin and yang in Do-In

For more advanced practitioners of Do-In it is the next step to bring yin and yang back into the practice in different ways. Below are a number of possibilities.

- Are you tired often? Then maybe you have been overactive (too yang) for a while. Then you should choose calm exercises for yin and yang meridians, to restore the yin quality in your life.
- When you feel anxious and are looking for peace, you can alternate between active (yang) exercises and peaceful (yin) exercises. You could also start out more actively and end very peacefully.
- You could also be tired because you haven't been cultivating enough yang. For example if you have been ill for a prolonged period. In that case start out with peaceful (yin) exercises and start complementing them with more and more active (yang) exercises.
- You can also adapt Do-In exercises to the temperature. If it is warm (yang) then quiet, stillness inducing and meditative exercises are more fitting (yin).
- If you notice that the front (yin) side of your body is very rigid, you can choose to do more exercises for the yin meridians to increase the flow of energy in this part of your body. You could alternately choose to emphasize the other side if you realize that the back of your body is especially stiff. Then you can perform more exercises for yang meridians.
- When you are cold, you can choose active (yang quality) exercises for the yang meridians, especially those that stimulate the Triple heater meridian.
- Yang meridians are weakened by wind, cold, heat, damp and dryness. Were you just soaked by rain, or where you sitting in a dry air conditioned room? Then put the emphasis on letting the yang meridians flow with Do-In exercises (please remove your soaking wet clothes first of course).
- If there is a specific yin meridian that you want to stimulate, then you should also stimulate the connected yang meridian. The yang meridians happen to amplify the yin meridians.
- If you want to reinforce a specific meridian, you can also use the five transformation system for that; check out Intermezzo 5 for that: *The cycle of life: the Five transformations.*
- The Chinese clock (see Intermezzo 6: Do-In and biorhythms: the Chinese clock) is a wonderful guideline for the order in which you choose to perform Do-In exercises. When you follow this clock, you automatically achieve a good balance in the series of exercises.
- Some people are sensitive to moon cycles. When it is full moon they don't sleep as well and their thoughts can be turbulent. If this applies to you, you can especially practice calming postures: choose slow exercises and focus on the yin meridians, especially those of Spleen, Lung and Kidney. During new moon, when a lot of people feel drained, you can pursue a more active practice of Do-In, for example with the full body massage and the back roll.

3 Spiritual development, joy, digestion, heart and blood vessels

Do-In for Heart and Small intestine

Getting acquainted with the meridians.

In this chapter you will find out along which pathway the meridians of Heart and Small intestine run, what their function is and which exercises you can do to balance them. This chapter starts with two exercises that stimulate these meridians and let you experience these energy channels right away.

Stretch for the Heart energy

Sit down on your hands and knees. Stretch out your arms and push your armpits down to the ground. The hips are held right above the knees. Feel the armpits and breast muscles stretch open. Stay in this position for five to ten breaths. The Heart meridian runs right along the path of the stretch that you feel in your armpits in this posture.

The Heart meridian originates in the armpit, then runs along the inside of your arm down to the cuticle of the pinky finger, on the side of your ring finger. A deeper running branch touches the heart and the small intestine. Another branch influences the throat, the tongue and the eyes.

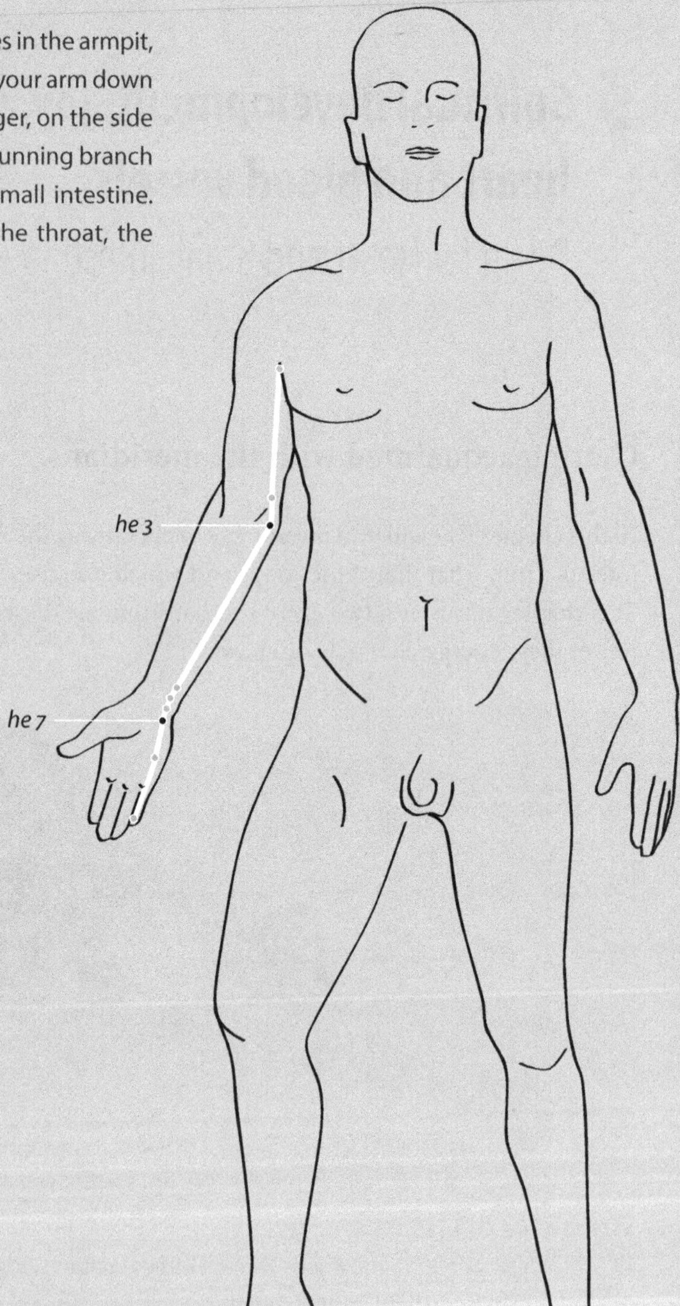

he 3

he 7

The Small intestine meridian originates on the outside of the cuticle of the pinky finger – across from the Heart meridian – and continues along the outside of the arm up to the shoulder, zigzagging over the shoulder blades. Then it runs upward along the neck and ends in the face closely in front of the ears. The internal branch of the meridian connects with the heart, the esophagus, the stomach and the small intestine.

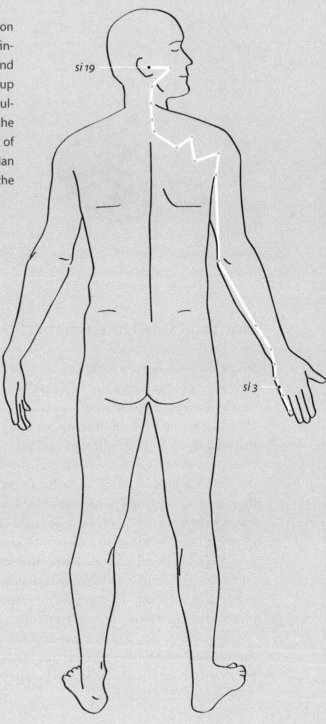

Stretch for the Small intestine energy

Sit down on your knees with your buttocks on your heels, bend forward and place your forehead on the ground. Interlace your fingers behind your back with the palms facing. Pull your shoulder blades toward each other. Stretch your arms and lift them towards the ceiling, or as far over your head as you can manage. Relax again after five calm and deep breaths and feel the muscles around the shoulder blades relax and become warmer. Repeat two more times. This posture helps you to dissolve stagnation in the Small intestine meridian, which in turn relaxes the shoulders and the upper back.

Heart and Small intestine: partners

In many different cultures the heart is seen as the seat of our soul or as a mirror to our feelings: the heart beats faster when we see our beloved or are very happy. But strong emotions are also sensed in a different part of our body: the belly (*hara* in Japanese). Just think of butterflies in your stomach when you are in love, or a stab to this area when you are startled. And it's not for nothing that we fold our hands over our belly when we feel insecure.

The connection between heart and small intestine is easily explained when you view this from the broader perspective that Chinese medicine attributes to the energy of these organs. The Heart governs the blood and blood vessels and plays a role in the transformation of the energy from our food into blood. Besides that the Heart energy processes the information that we ingest through our senses and transforms these into a reaction. The Small intestine filters our nutrition (the building blocks for amongst others blood). The information which is transferred to us by our senses, can also be seen as a form of nutrition. The energy of the Small intestine in turn determines which impressions from the senses that the Heart needs to address and which ones it can neglect.

Only after the Small intestine energy has 'previewed' these impressions, they will end up with the heart. In this way the Heart – which is seen as the emperor of the body – isn't unnecessarily overloaded by our emotions. Furthermore the small intestine disperses our mental energy.

Heart and Small intestine are also associated with heat, transformation, movement, excitement and susceptibility.

Joy

The emotion that is connected to the Heart, is joy. This also includes the feeling of enjoying to do something for another without expecting anything back. On the other hand incessant laughter, or laughing at inappropriate moments is a sign of imbalance.

The negative energy of the heart expresses itself in anxiety. There are people that always have to be doing something and when they finally are sitting down, for example during a dinner party, are always fidgeting with the cutlery or the table cloth. This is a sign of an imbalance in the Heart energy.

Bitter

The Dutch expression 'bitter in the mouth makes the heart healthy' also is true according to Eastern medicine. The meridians of Heart and Small intestine are reinforced with roasted food and products that have a bitter taste, such as Brussels sprouts, chicory and arugula. But also with tastes there must be a balance: extreme preference for a specific taste points towards an imbalance. When the meridians of heart and small intestine are out of balance, you probably prefer black coffee, Campari and bitter chocolate. If there is truly an imbalance, then besides that you might often have a bitter taste in your mouth.

What does the Heart energy do?

The Heart meridian nourishes the heart, which gives it the energy to pump the blood round. Besides that the Heart energy assists in producing blood, controlling the blood vessels and processing the emotions that the other organs were unable to and have sent forward to the Heart. The Heart energy is often compared to the head of state: who leaves the daily running of the government over to the ministers and only applies himself to the most important of subjects. Especially in ancient times the wellbeing of the head of state was important to the stability of a country. Therefore he was not bothered with too many questions.

In our body the same applies: only if you are burdened with emotional problems for prolonged periods of time the Heart energy will be addressed. If this continues for longer than a few months, the heart function suffers from this.

The Heart is also the place where consciousness dwells, *shen* (*shin* in Japanese). This is how the balance of the energy determines our higher spiritual potential: pure consciousness means that we do not judge or form attachment to ideas or material things. And when there is no more attachment to personality, status, opinions etc., there is more space for our spiritual and mental capacities to let us live our true destiny. This leads to what is called enlightenment in Buddhism and in yoga is referred to as Samadhi: a calm state of happiness.

What do you experience when your Heart energy is imbalanced?
Disturbances in the Heart energy often are connected to an accumulation of tension, alarm or fatigue. The complaints which then arise, mostly express themselves in the vicinity of the branches of the Heart meridian: the eye, the tongue, the diaphragm and the small intestine. The following complaints often present themselves when there is an imbalance in this energy. If you recognize a number of these, then you can put emphasis on exercises for the Heart meridian in your practice.

Physical:
- Heart problems and/or palpitations
- Problems with sleeping, insomnia
- Dry mouth
- Blood tends to flow to the head
- Tension in the tongue and because of this stuttering or stammering
- Pain in the upper back
- Curved upper back (due to weak abdominal muscles)
- Shock, coma, delirium
- Short memory combined with fears and palpitations
- Shortness of breath
- Restriction and severe pain in the chest (angina pectoris)
- Feeling of tension or restriction directly under the sternum (breastbone)
- Abundant sweating: moist palms, armpits or feet
- Fidgety hands
- Unable to stop talking
- Insufficient circulation

Mental:
- Agitation, nervous, skittish
- Incapable of calming yourself

- Constant sense of bitterness
- Inappropriate laughter
- Emotional fatigue following crisis or abundant stress
- Paranoid feelings and or schizophrenia

What does the Small intestine energy do?

The small intestine is a digestive channel between the stomach and the large intestine. The wall of the intestine secretes enzymes for the digestion and absorbs the nutrition that has been broken down. The Eastern view on the small intestine is that it also takes the mental digestion into account. These are processes that take place outside our realm of consciousness in our daily life. When the meridian is balanced, the energy of the Small intestine ingests the emotions; if the meridian is overloaded – and that can also be from emotions – then often intestinal complaints arise. That is the reason that many people during a busy or emotionally taxing period develop upset stomachs, including diarrhea, constipation or irritable bowel syndrome (spastic colon). Very sensitive people experience this on a daily basis.

Besides this the energy of the Small intestine helps us to have a low point of gravity in our belly. A lot of stressful brainwork – which gives the Small intestine energy a lot of mental material to digest – coincides with superficial breathing and decreases the natural contractions (peristalsis) of the bowel. This is also what creates different stomach complaints such as spastic colon.

What do you experience when the Small intestine energy is out of balance?
Problems pertaining to the Small intestine meridian often come from being frightened or suppressing emotions. Symptoms that frequently present themselves for an imbalance in the Small intestine are listed below.

Physical:
- Easily fatigued
- Pain in the neck, shoulders and/or elbows
- Leg cramps
- Irregular bowel movements
- Diarrhea or contrarily constipation
- Abdominal pain combined with thirst, dark urine and/or restlessness

- Bubbling in the stomach
- Distended belly
- Bad digestion and because of that skinny and/or lack of energy
- Flabby or loose flesh
- Cold legs and abdomen combined with a hot face
- Burning urine and insomnia after emotional problems
- Thin or contrarily swollen lower lip

Mental:
- Feelings being overruled by thoughts
- Not experiencing appreciation for what you have achieved
- Suppressing unpleasant emotions
- The wish to not be surpassed/beaten
- Introverted, clumsy behavior

Exercises for Heart and Small intestine energy

The meridians of the Heart and Small intestine are located right next to each other. That is why some of the stretches will affect both of them simultaneously. The following exercises are examples that show you how to reinforce the energy of the Heart and Small intestine.

Linking hands

Seat yourself in a cross-legged position with your right leg on top of the other. Now fold your right leg – if possible – further over your left leg, in a way that aligns both knees above each other. The insteps of your feet are touching the ground. This is a kind of exaggerated cross-legged position. If this pose feels uncomfortable for the knees, then you can stretch out your left leg.

Extend your right arm upwards, bend it and position the hand between your shoulder blades. Then bend the left arm and bring it behind your back. Try to link the fingers of your left and right hand and hook them together. If you can't reach this way, 'help' the upper elbow with the other hand, or hold a towel or a shawl between your hands. In time you will be able to inch worm your hands together closer and closer, or even make this aid obsolete. Relax after five to ten calm breaths and also do the exercise on the other side.

Effect: In this posture you feel the stretch through the sides of the upper arm, where the meridians of the Heart and Small intestines run; this relaxes the upper arms and helps with headaches and insomnia. In the legs you are lightly stretching the yin meridians, as well as one of the extraordinary vessels, and also the Masunaga-branche of the small intestine, which strengthens sexuality, relaxes the groin as well as tension in the lower back.

Propeller

Sit on your knees (*seiza*), or in another comfortable position, such as the cross-legged position.

hook the fingers of your hands in front of your abdomen. Alternate the elbows up and down to the rhythm of your breath. The shoulders softly follow the movement. Repeat ten times.

Effect: This movement loosens the Small intestine meridian in your arms and shoulders and therefore relaxes the shoulders and the upper back; it helps you to breathe deeper, which also relaxes the belly.

Relaxing the upper back for Heart and Small intestine

Sit down on your buttocks. Place the soles of the feet together and pull them towards you as close as you can. Let your knees open to the sides. Stretch your back, so that you feel your sit bones on the floor. Wrap your hands around your feet with your left hand over your right hand, without tugging on the toes. This symbolises yang (left hand) above yin (right hand), as heaven is above earth.

Bow your head towards your feet. You no longer have to keep your back stretched, you are allowed to bend it. Relax your shoulders and relax your arms. The force of gravity is strong enough to give you a stretch. Return to upright position after five to ten calm breaths.

Effect: This exercise relaxes your upper back around the area of the heart and the muscles along your shoulder blades, where the Small intestine meridian runs, it relaxes the whole back and stimulates the flow throughout the belly.

Empty the heart

'Empty the heart, bring peace to the mind', is an expression by Chinese philosopher Lao Tse. To totally bring peace to your mind, you adopt a meditative pose (*seiza*, cross-legged position or on a chair) with a straight back and you follow your breath for at least a quarter of an hour. You do not have to try anything or actively engage. Just be, sit, breathe and be observant to whatever presents itself.

Do not try to adopt an elevated or spiritual inner attitude, or try too hard. You don't have to do anything extra, except take the time to experience the 'now'. The Buddha called each form of longing a reason for suffering. Or put differently: longing is a distraction from the state experiencing happiness. This means that even if you try very hard to meditate, you will only be kept away from the meditation and the sense of inner happiness. The real art in this practice is therefore to be relaxed and attentive without ever wanting to achieve anything.

Effect: This is a really good exercise to start or end the day with. This strengthens your attention and concentration throughout the day and brings you peace in the evening, which in turn will lead to a wonderful night of sleep.

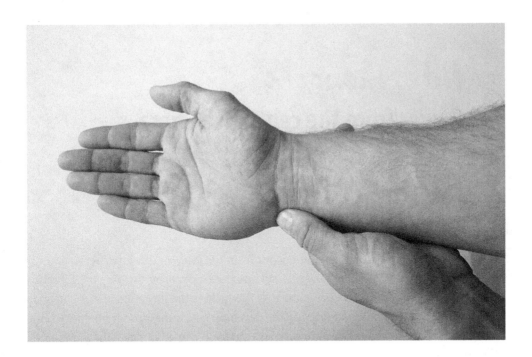

Calm

Find the crease on the inside of your right wrist on the pinky side. Press your left thumb into the spot on this crease which is aligned with the pinky finger, just besides the two tendons in the middle of the wrist (*the name of this point is Path to happiness, gate of consciousness*). Apply gentle pressure. This pressure point is on the Heart meridian and has a calming effect for all kinds of stress, it also clears the mind. After a few minutes you can change sides.

Painful points

When a meridian is blocked, the *tsubo's* (pressure points) on the meridian become painful and hard, even before the organ connected to the meridian becomes diseased. Self applied acupressure or massage to a pressure point soothes and lets the energy in that location flow once again. Within days the same point can become sensitive again. It is possible that the meridian stagnates due to an external influence such as stress, wind, cold, dryness, dampness or wrong nutrition. Sometimes the meridian becomes blocked elsewhere. Through stretches, massage and a healthy lifestyle, with regular practice the blockage can be dissolved.

Intermezzo 3
Power from the center: the hara

The second brain

Make your practice more effective and work from the *hara*; in this intermezzo you will read all about what *hara* is and how you can integrate it while performing the exercises.

In the East they act on the principle that the belly is the power center of our body. This is the reason why Joseph Pilates, while developing his fitness program – which was also partially inspired by the Eastern martial arts – also named this area the *powerhouse*. The Japanese have named this area *hara* for centuries.

In the *hara*, the area between the ribcage and the pubic bone, the process of digestion takes place. This area in the body is the source of our daily energy, and also the source of construction material for the various tissues in our body. When the *hara* does not perform properly, we do not derive sufficient energy from our nutrition to preserve our self healing vitality.

But to view the *hara* purely as the main center of our digestive tract is a blunt oversimplification. This area of your body mirrors your mental, emotional and physical condition. We can all relate to the sensation of intense emotions in our belly such as a stab, butterflies, tension, warmth or cold. This language of the *hara* has been extensively researched in Japan, so it is even possible for shiatsu therapist to feel from the *hara* which energy channel they should treat and which emotions are overly present in a person.

Besides this the *hara* is also recognized as our ideal center of gravity: many Japanese and Chinese work out to strengthen their *hara*. Which means, they practice moving their center of gravity under their belly button – the center of the *hara*. This area of the abdomen is also referred to as 'the second brain' or the 'sensate brain'. If you live from this center, you feel more healthy and balanced. It also offers stability, calmness and strength, peace and concentration, which also comes in handy with martial arts, but also during Zen meditation or cultural arts such as flower arrangement (Ikebana) and calligraphy. Performance of all these arts is always preceded by a few moments of concentrating on the *hara*.

Those who live from the hara, *stand strong (low center of gravity). Those who live from the head, have a high center of gravity and are easily destabilized.*

Hara in Do-In

Now that you have read through the first chapters, it is time to add an extra dimension onto your Do-In practice, because you are meant, just as with all Japanese disciplines, to also perform each Do-In exercise from the *hara*. So up until a few moments ago for those who had no idea what *hara* was, this might sound more complicated than it really it. The idea behind this is to simply imagine that the strength to perform each exercise, originates from the belly. Because body and mind are united, the power of imagination is very strong. You could on top of that imagine your lower belly as the center of a three dimensional circle with a diameter of about 1,5 meter.

Initially it can be very challenging to (dare to) move from the *hara* and not to pull in your belly. It is after all the idea of beauty as the norm to have the flattest possible tummy. But a strong *hara* is not exactly the same as having rock solid abs or pulling in your tummy. When you pull your belly in, you are just moving your blood and organs upward. Effectively moving your center of gravity up, thus making you less stable and grounded. This is the direct opposite of *hara*.

A relaxed but powerful *hara* however has many benefits – also besides the times that you are practicing Do-In or yoga (in yoga the power of the *hara* is called *core* strength). For example if you breath deep into the abdomen during a challenging conversation, you stand more firmly, you seem more calm and convincing and your face will not redden as easily. If someone bumps into you, you will not be as easily pushed out of balance if you were standing or walking from your *hara*.

Moving from your *hara*

Imagine riding a bicycle. When you stick out your arm to signal and look to the side, you still move straight forward. But what would happen if you turn your abdomen (*hara*) to the right as well? In that instant the direction you are cycling in changes and you make a right turn. Only when your abdomen changes direction, your body will follow.

Exercises to strengthen the *hara*

The next three exercises are quite different, but all three of them strengthen our center. This shows that there are many ways and moments that you could apply this. The massage exercise from Part 2, chapter 1, *Self shiatsu: massage to promote the flow of energy* is also beneficial to the *hara*.

Sea of energy

The center of the hara, where all of our power originates from, is called *Tan Den* (Japanese) or *Tan'tien* or *Dantian* (Chinese). This refers to the innermost deep part of the belly, about 1,5 thumb-width under the bellybutton. This spot is also a *tsubo* and has two frequently referred to names which are Ki Kai (sometimes spelled Ki Kei) or Conception vessel 6. The translation of Ki Kai is 'Sea of energy', which is to say the storage facility for our basic energy.

To increase your energy, press lightly on the Ki Kai for ten minutes while breathing deep into the abdomen. To find this point you place your fingers parallel to the navel with the index finger on the midline. The point exactly under the ring finger is where it is located. If this point is sensitive, you can also warm it by placing your palm over it.

Balloon

Seat yourself comfortably, for example in *seiza*, or in cross-legged position. Close your eyes, lower your shoulders into relaxation, relax your abdomen and also relax the small muscles in your face.

Imagine your torso as a balloon. During each breathe the balloon is filled with air. Feel the center from which your belly expands in all directions. This is the *hara* center. It is not important to be able to point out a specific location in the belly, you only have to experience and feel. Breath in and out deliberately for at least one minute while focusing on your center.

Duo *hara* enhancer

It is best to perform this exercise with two people. The first person is seated on hands and knees with the hands directly under the shoulders, knees directly under the hips. This person is the first to strengthen the *hara*. The second person supports by standing behind the other and placing the hands on the lower back of the person who is standing on hands and knees.

During inhalation the first person arches the back. The second person follows the movement without exerting any pressure. During the exhalation the first person rounds out the back by pushing the underbelly upwards and pulling in the belly button actively. The second person exerts counter pressure on the back with the hands. This is followed by yet another relaxed inhalation without pressure from the second person. Be aware of not pushing out the breath in one blow during this exercise but focusing on keeping a calm and evenly flowing breath.

This exercise strengthens the *hara* and the Kidneys of the person on hands and knees. The exercise will warm up the lower back. This exercise is most powerful with a partner supporting the back, but can also be performed as a solo exercise. After ten breaths you change places with your partner.

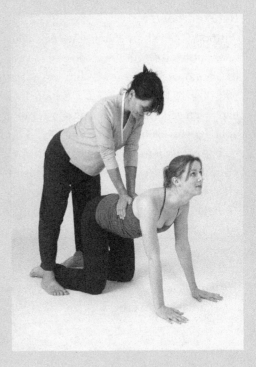

Relaxed power

Position yourself on your back. Bend your knees and raise your lower legs; the lower legs are now parallel to the ground. Place your hands on your upper legs. Push your legs away with your hands. Simultaneously press your lower back into the ground and your tailbone away from you. Keep your knees in position with the power of your center. Relax after two full breaths. Repeat three times.

This exercise strengthens the *hara* and pacifies the psoas muscle. This muscle contracts under stress. It arches the back. In many people this muscle is continuously contracted. This can lead to complaints in the whole lower body.

'*Real medicine is practiced as soon as the doctor places his hand on the patients hara.*'
— Shiatsu proverb

4 Will-power, life force energy, fertility and a flexible back
Do-In for Kidneys and Bladder

Getting acquainted with the meridians

Discover where the Kidney and Bladder meridian runs, what their function is and which exercises let the energy flow freely. This chapter starts off with two exercises which stimulate these meridians so you can immediately experience these energy channels.

Stretch for Bladder energy

Start out sitting on the ground with both legs stretched out in front of you. Pull your toes towards you and let them face upwards, so there is already a slight stretch along the back of your legs. Lengthen your back, especially the lower back. Feel that you are on top of your sit bones. If necessary bend your legs if this helps you to lengthen your spine, of sit on a small pillow. Now flex yourself forwards from the hips. Place your hands on your shins, ankles or feet. Stay in this position for five to ten calm breaths. Experience that there is still room for deep breathing, even if the body is doubled over. In this position you feel a stretch in the back of your legs and along your spine through the Bladder meridian; the Kidney meridian is also stretched in this position.

The Bladder meridian originates at the inner corner of the eyes near the bridge of the nose, runs over the head and splits itself into two branches which each run parallel to the spine over the long dorsal muscle. The meridian continues its path over the back of the leg, behind the ankle and ends at the pinky toe. The Bladder meridian has a deeper branch through the brain, kidneys and bladder.

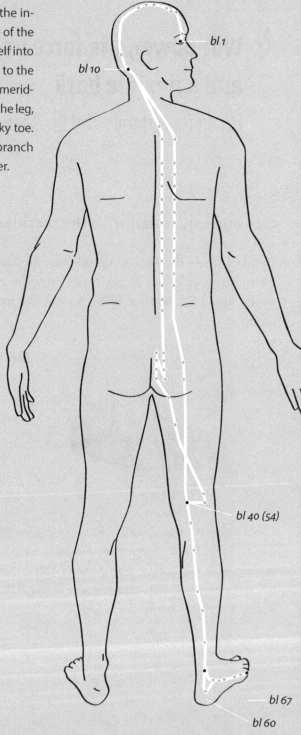

bl 1

bl 10

bl 40 (54)

bl 67

bl 60

The Kidney meridian originates on the sole of the foot and runs along the inside of the ankle and along the back of the inner leg up to the groin. From this point up the meridian continues along the front of the torso, up in a straight line, just alongside the midline, to the clavicle. The Kidney meridian influences the lumbar vertebrae, kidneys, bladder, liver, throat, ears and tongue through deeper running branches. Besides this the Kidney meridian governs the deep-seated tissues of our body such as bones and marrow.

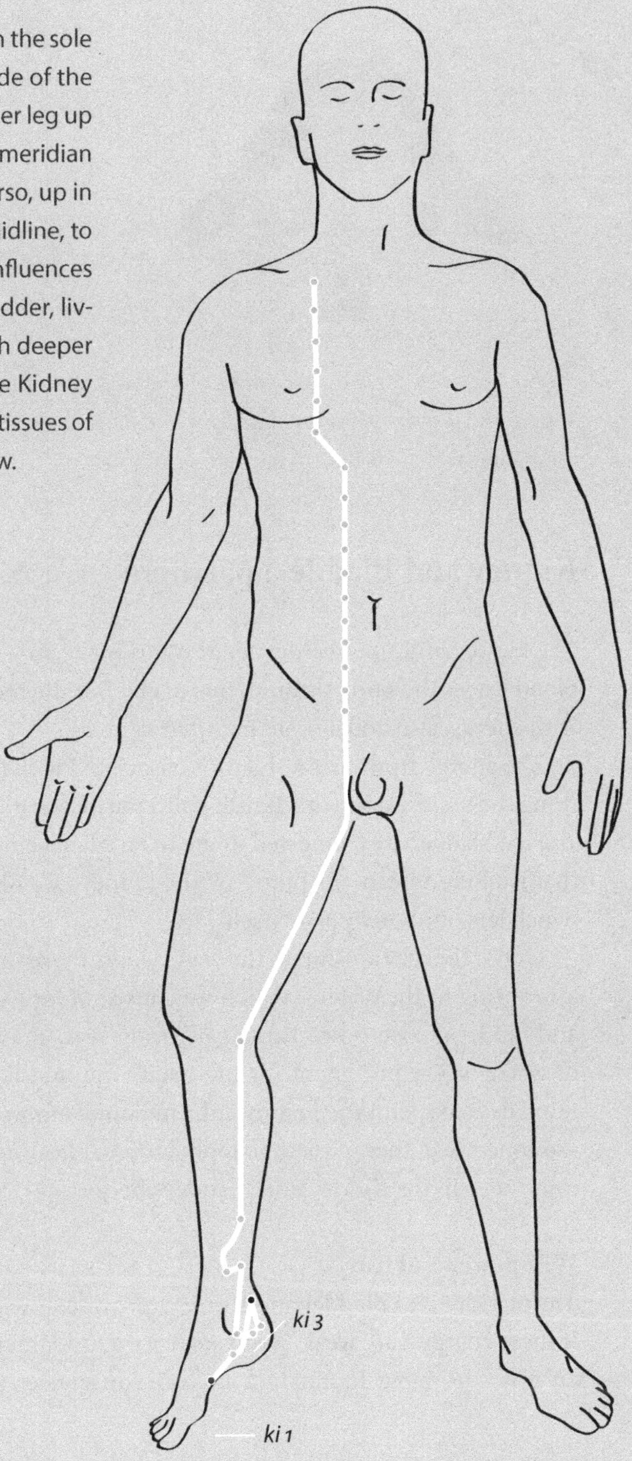

ki 3

ki 1

Stretch for the Kidney energy

Stand in straddle pose, toes slightly pointing towards each other and heels outwards. Bend forward with a straight back and place your hands under your shoulders on the ground. Push your heels to the backwards and out keeping them in place. Hold your shoulder-blades together on your back. In this position you can feel the Kidney meridian on the inside of your legs. After five to ten calm breaths you can return back to an upright position.

You should avoid positions where the head hangs lower than the hips in cases of hypertension (high blood pressure).

Kidney and Bladder: partners

The kidney and the bladder team up to make sure that the waste material from our blood leaves the body through our urine. But the meridians that provide these organs with energy, also collaborate in different areas.

The energy from these organs is associated with life, fluidity, strength and purification. The association with fluidity and purification is quite clear, because the kidneys and the bladder are connected to the water management in our body. Through the urine that is filtered from our blood by the kidneys we obviously eliminate waste material, which lets our body purify itself.

Out of the relationship to the waterworks the associations with fertility and strength also spring forth. Water – which we consist of for 65 percent – after all is not only soft and fluid, but also powerful: it can erode away mountains. Besides that the presence of water is a requirement for life itself. The first life forms originated in water, and humans also spend the first months in liquid: amniotic fluid. Where fertility problems are concerned, therapists that apply Oriental healing therefore often stumble upon an imbalance in the Kidney and Bladder energy.

Will-power and fear

The meridians of Bladder and Kidneys provide us with perseverance and the vital urge. If these energies are weak, we experience a fundamental type of fear. This type of anxiety arises from our foundation and can run so deep that we (unconsciously or without reason) can experience a fear of losing our life. Sometimes this feeling produces a form of will-power: an iron determination or unwillingness to give up.

People that are prone to fears, will benefit from preserving their Kidney energy. The most important changes in daily life that can influence this are a good night's sleep, reduction of stress, avoiding alcohol and drugs and eating food that fits with the season you are in. Furthermore several types of therapy, breathing exercises and calm Do-In exercises are helpful in managing fear.

Seasonal products

According to Eastern healing philosophy our environment offers us exactly what we need in each season. In summer the regional products are refreshing vegetables and fruit for example, like strawberries and cucumbers. These refresh and cool us in the hottest period of the year. In winter it is more the various types of cabbage and carrots that are available. These wintery products posses a warming effect, exactly what we need in this time of year. Eating an abundance of cooling products in winter depletes the *ki*, especially that of the Kidneys. Those who mostly eat cold meals with lots of raw vegetables in winter, can provide themselves with more energy and resistance by putting more warm seasonal products on their menu.

What does the Kidney energy do?

The Kidney meridian provides the energy for the kidneys and the adrenal glands to keep the composition of the blood at a constant level. One of the things these organs do is leveling out blood pressure and blood sugar levels. To achieve this they filter out salts, sugars and waste products from our blood. All these materials are eliminated in the form of urine.

To perform their tasks, the kidneys produce several hormones. Part of these hormones assist in filtering the blood. Other hormones influence our reactions to stress and the ability to recover from this, so we do not exhaust ourselves. The kidneys also produce the male and female sexual hormones; this is one of the primary reasons that these organs are associated with fertility and reproduction.

Our left kidney is also referred to as the Water Kidney. This tends to keep the left side of our body from overheating from the warmth that the heart produces. The right kidney is referred to as the Fire Kidney. It warms the right side of our body.

The Kidney energy also expresses itself through the ears and provides clear hearing. You can literally tell from an ear if someone has been provided with strong Kidney energy at birth: big fleshy ears that have a healthy blood supply (but not with burst capillaries) are a sign of healthy Kidney energy and a strong constitution. The Kidney energy weakens as we grow older, as well as the hearing – an expression of the Kidney energy – which declines with age.

Sources of energy

According to Eastern healing philosophy our parents provide us with part of our energy, from the sperm and egg which we originate from. This energy, the *prenatal energy*, is stored in our Kidneys. Within this prenatal energy which is stored in our center, the hara, the foundation of our being is incorporated; both in a physical as well as in an energetic sense. Our constitution is determined by this. Each day we use a little of this prenatal energy. When we die, we have consumed the total supply.

The prenatal energy from the Kidney is mixed with the energy that we produce ourselves. The *postnatal ki* is derived from our nutrition and the air, that is the reason why Do-In and other forms of healing exercises put such emphasis on proper breathing and nutrition. The more postnatal *ki* we produce, the less prenatal *ki* we need and the stronger the chance is that we live long and in good health. Those who breathe superficially, eat poorly or maybe even both, are not able to produce much postnatal *ki*. Therefore he or she will consume more prenatal *ki*.

Salt

Legumes (especially aduki beans and kidney beans, preferably dried and not canned), seaweed and fish provide energy for the kidneys. Tip: the cooking liquid from these beans also strengthens the kidneys. Save it and use it in soup the next day. The slightly salty taste from fish and seaweed retain fluids, which in limited amounts is good for us. Too much salt makes the body rigid and dehydrates it. This makes us drink excessively which leads to more work for the kidneys. This happens at the expense of the Kidney energy.

What do you experience when the Kidney function is imbalanced?

An imbalance in Kidney energy often results from an exhausting lifestyle (which is most easily resolved by adapting your lifestyle). Dark bagginess under the eyes, a sign of fatigue, are a clue to a decreased Kidney energy. This will lead to the following summary of complaints.

Physical:
- Black or blue shades over the face
- Edema
- Hearing problems
- Prostate problems
- Frequent nightly urination
- Abundant or sparse urination
- Impotence
- Exaggerated or weak sexual activity
- Pain in the lumbar region (low back)
- Weak or frail bones
- Heaviness in the head from lack of sleep
- High blood pressure from diminished renal function (renal hypertension)
- Perspiration in hands and face
- Frequent stumbling
- Split ends in the hair
- Hot soles of the feet
- Infertility

Mental:
- An unfounded sense that your life is at stake
- Lack of will-power
- Fear – often about what the future will bring
- Extreme valor (a preference to extreme sports)
- Working compulsively
- Dementia
- Oversensitive to noise
- Experiencing too much stress

What does the Bladder meridian do?

Obviously the Bladder meridian influences the urinary bladder, a type of balloon in the lower abdomen which collects the urine from the kidneys and gives us the urge to make our way to the toilet in a timely fashion. The function of the meridian is broader. The Bladder meridian is one of the longest energy channels in the body and is connected to all the other organs through the *tsubo's* (acu-points) on the back. This implies that through the Bladder meridian it is possible to influence all other organs, including the emotions that these organs and their meridians are associated with. At the same time an imbalance in an organ for the most part is always noticeable in the back. It will distort or become rigid.

In the East there is a saying that the flexibility of the back discloses the true age of the body: a flexible and strong back show that someone is young, healthy and full of life. This increases the likelihood of many more healthy years. People are startled by this Eastern proverb, because they do not find themselves particularly limber and suspect that they are probably physically very old. Looking at this from the bright side: the back can become more flexible through exercising, which means you are still able to rejuvenate yourself at a respectably high age!

What do you experience when the Bladder meridian is imbalanced?

Because the Bladder meridian runs along the spine, it is a major influence on our posture, literally and figuratively. Psychologically the Bladder energy represents our 'backbone' and our determination. Problems connected to the Bladder meridian often have to do with exhaustion. Common symptoms connected to an imbalance of the Bladder are listed below.

Physical:
- Abundant and clear urine or on the contrary little and dark/muddy urine
- Frequent urination
- Cystitis (bladder infection)
- Painful periods (menstruation)
- Infertility
- Distortion of the back
- Lumbar pain (lower back)
- Sciatica
- Having trouble with back bending
- Nasal congestion

- Abundant sweating
- Overly sensitive to cold.

Mental:
- Nervous
- Simple irritations become sources of stress
- Startled easily
- Always having a sense of time pressure/deadline
- Fatigue and lack of motivation
- Jealousy
- Suspicion
- Obsessions

Exercises to balance the Kidney and Bladder energy

The meridians of Bladder and Kidney are situated near each other. Because of this a posture is usually beneficial to both of the meridians. The following exercises improve the flow of energy in the meridians of Kidney and Bladder. Other exercises that also stretch the back of your legs and your back, are beneficial to the Kidneys and the Bladder.

Head to knee

Sit on the ground with your legs stretched out and place your right heel against the inside of your left thigh, as close to your groin as possible. Lower the right knee towards the ground. Turn your body slightly towards your left leg. On an exhale bend forward and grab hold of your left foot or shin – you could also hook a scarf around your foot and hold onto it with both hands. Pull the toes of that foot towards you and push the heel away. Bring yourself back to an upright position after five to ten deep and calm breaths. Change over to the other leg and repeat the exercise.

Effect: In this posture you stretch the Bladder and the Kidney meridian in your straight leg. This opens the meridians, enhances circulation of the leg and relaxes the lower back.

Duo bend

Perform this exercise with a partner. This way you help each other to relax more deeply. Start sitting back to back with legs stretched out. The first person bends forward, keeping the toes straight towards the ceiling. Then the second person leans back and stretches out the arms along the ears whilst being supported by the back of the first partner. If needed the second partner can place a pillow under the neck. After five to ten calm breaths you can change positions.

Effect: In this exercise you heat up each other's back, and specifically in the area of the kidneys. This – combined with the extra weight – helps the bottom partner to bend further forward. The top partner experiences a stretch that opens the torso which amongst other things opens the Kidney meridian.

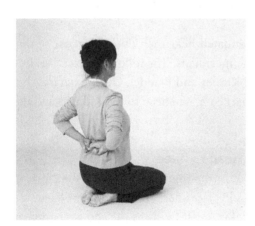

Rubbing

Sit cross-legged or in *seiza* (on bent knees) and place your hands on your lower back – the area of the kidneys. Now start rubbing vigorously over your lower back so that it warms up. After that leave your hands on your back for a minute, so the heat can penetrate inward.

Effect: This exercise is beneficial to the Kidneys and relaxes the lower back.

Ginger oil

Would you like to pamper your Kidneys a little more? Then rub your back with a massage oil that contains essential oil of ginger before you start this exercise. Ginger provides extra heat and energy. It is easy to make this oil yourself. Use one part of juice from grated ginger root with one part of almond or sesame oil. Or buy essential oil of ginger at a health food store and mix this according to the instructions with for example almond oil. Some people are allergic to ginger, so try out which effect this has on you with a small amount of oil first.

Relaxed neck

Start out in cross-legged position. Let your head hang down, if you experience that this is already a pretty good stretch, then this is as far as it goes. Then place your hands on the back of your head and let the elbows hang down. After five to ten breaths you release the hands and return your head to an upright position.

Effect: Due to the force of gravity a stretch is achieved in the part of the Bladder meridian that runs along the neck and spine. This relaxes the neck and upper back.

Relaxed lower back

Lie down on your back. Bend your legs and place the feet on the floor right behind your buttocks. Place your hands under your sacrum (the heart shaped bone at the bottom of your spine). Touch the tops of the thumbs and index fingers together. These fingers now form a triangle around the sacrum. Arch your back while you inhale and round your back on the exhale. Repeat this for at least one minute. You are massaging the sacrum.

Effect: On and around this bone there are several *tsubo's* belonging to the Bladder meridian. Massaging this area balances tranquility and activity, relaxes the lower back and alleviates menstrual pain.

Intermezzo 4
Powerless or tension: kyo and jitsu

Working the imbalance

After having performed the exercises from the earlier chapters, you might have experienced that some movements come easier to you than others. And for the exercises that you have performed first on the right and then on the left (such as the head to knee exercise in the last chapter), you might have experienced that right and left do not feel the same at all.

The rigid side is referred to as *jitsu*, which could be translated as 'full' or 'tense'. This side relatively holds too much energy and therefore is hard and not so flexible. The flexible side is referred to as *kyo*, which means 'empty' or maybe even 'powerless'. This side does not hold enough energy. *kyo* and *jitsu* therefore could also be seen as the areas of the body that are relatively yin or are yang.

The areas that are *jitsu*, are hard and often stick out. The shiatsu therapist named Masunaga represented this as viewing the energy body as a perfect round ball. If there was a lump on the ball somewhere, this spot could be viewed as *jitsu*. A dent in the ball would represent *kyo*.

Easy side first

Areas that are *jitsu*, such as tense hard shoulders, are obvious because of heat, tension or bulging. It is however important to understand that the areas that are *kyo* are the cause of the problem. If you notice that while performing an exercise there is a clear difference between one or the other side, you always begin with the *kyo*-side, so that would be the side that feels the easiest to you. (Even if an exercise in this book asks you to perform the right side first, you will start out on the left if this is your *kyo*-side). This way you are showing your body which side needs the extra energy.

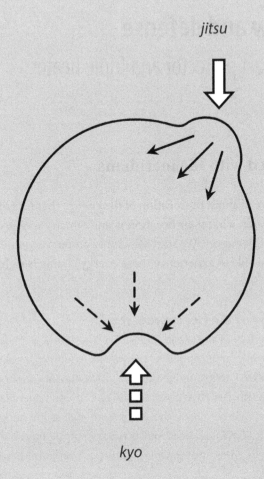

jitsu

kyo

After this you perform the exercise on the *jitsu* side. This way you stimulate the body to redistribute the excess energy from the *jitsu* side, thus creating more balance and in the end an almost unperceivable difference between left and right, front and back.

Because the body also always aims for balance, you will experience that – given the choice – you almost always intuitively choose the *kyo*-side first.

5 Blood flow and defense
Do-In for Heart protector and Triple heater

Getting acquainted with the meridians

In this chapter you will read about the location of the energy channels of the Heart protector and the Triple heater, what their function is and which exercises help to let you bring enhanced flow to this energy. We start off with two exercises which will stimulate the meridians so you are able to experience these energy channels right away.

Stretch for the energy of the Heart protector

Sit in *seiza* (on folded knees) or in cross-legged position. Interlace your fingers and push the tips of both thumbs and pinky fingers together. Lift your arms with your palms facing up and if possible stretch your elbows – this sounds easier than it is. Relax and let your shoulders drop while you bring your hands up as high as possible, and hold the shoulder blades together on the back; this keeps the muscles between the shoulder as well as the neck relaxed. Make a little roof out of your hands above your head, pulling your wrists slightly apart to achieve this. Breathe in and out calmly five times, and then relax. In this position you are stretching the Heart protector meridian.

The Heart protector meridian surfaces in the pectoral muscles, close to the nipple. It runs along the biceps on the inside of the arm, along the center of the elbow, forearm and wrist over the palm of the hand to the outside of the middle finger. A branch of the meridian runs over the chest to the heart and pericardium (heart sac), this part descends internally through the diaphragm to the lower belly. The meridian thus is connected to the three 'heaters' which integrate the meridian of the Triple heater. You will read more about these three heaters later in this chapter.

The Triple heater meridian orginates at the cuticle of the ring finger, on the side of the pinky finger. It runs along the ring finger, over the back of the hand and then continues along the outside of the arm, right across from the Heart protector meridian. After that around the shoulder, along the side of the neck, around the ear towards the temples. On the shoulder the energy channel touches the Small intestine meridian and the Governing vessel. Internally the meridian runs down, and on the chest it connects to the energy channel of the Heart protector and thus connects this channel with the three 'heaters'.

he p 6

he p 8

Stretch for the energy of the Triple heater

Following the last exercise you reverse the position of the hands so that the backs face upwards. Relax your shoulders while you stretch out your arms as far as you can. You will primarily feel the stretch in the forearms. Bend your body to the left and right to also give the upper arms a mild stretch as well. Relax after five to ten calm breaths. In this position you are stretching the Triple heater meridian, especially the area near the wrists.

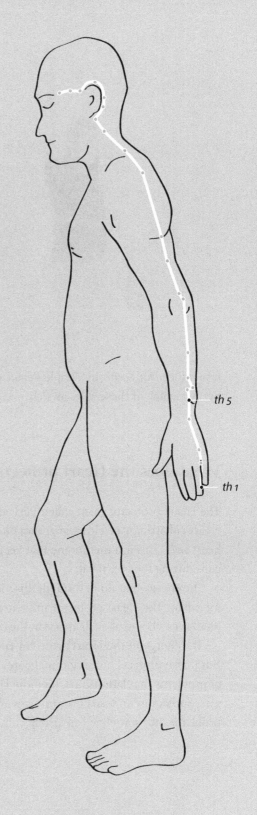

th 5

th 1

Heart protector and Triple heater: partners

The heart is such an important organ, that multiple energy channels take care of its regulations and protection. Those are the channels of the Small intestine, Heart protector and the Triple heater. All three of them filter out information before it reaches the Heart, much like a suit of armor. The subtlety lies herein that the Small intestine is more focused on nutrition (so that none of the wrong materials end up in our bloodstream), it distincts pure from impure also with mental inputs. With the Heart protector the focus is on emotions (so the heart is not exhausted by our emotional life). And with the Triple heater the focus is on thoughts, but all three of them perform each of these roles as well.

What does the Heart protector energy do?

The Heart protector (also called Pericardium, Circulation meridian, Circulation sex, Heart constrictor or Heart governor) has a true physical form as the pericardium (or heart sac). This is a membrane that keeps the heart from rubbing up against other organs during the heartbeat.

The energy that flows through this meridian has just as many functions as the Heart meridian. The Heart protector influences the heart, the major blood vessels, the lymphatic vessels and as such assists in the central circulation of blood and lymphatic fluid.

The energy of the Heart protector conveys the will of the Heart energy to the body. But it also protects our emotional core. When this is threatened, especially in the case of problems in relationships, then the Heart protector comes up with defensive strategies. Someone can transform into a workaholic, so there is no more time for personal problems. But someone can also become truly sensitive and exhibit extreme behavior, through which this demanding or aggressive attitude covers up the vulnerability of the Heart.

Also complete absence of emotion can be a sign of an imbalance in the Heart protector meridian.

Because this energy protects the Heart, it also provides the stability of *shen*, the awareness. So in case of mental excitement, worries and other situations that need pacifying, choose Do-In exercises for this meridian.

What do you experience when there is an imbalance in the Heart protector energy?

Because the energy executes the commands of the Heart, the symptoms of an imbalance are almost the same as those of the Heart energy. The following list covers complaints that regularly occur with an imbalance of the heart protector.

Physical:
- Delirium
- Epilepsy
- Coma
- Ulcers on the tongue
- High fever
- Insomnia
- Problems with the heart
- Pain in the chest
- Sweaty hands and feet, cold sweat on the chest
- A sensation of mist in the head
- Exhaustion due to over-concentration
- Rapid heart rate
- Abnormal blood pressure
- Tightness and severe pain in the chest (angina pectoris)
- Shortness of breath
- Sensitive sternum (breastbone)
- Sensitive pectoral muscles
- Obsession with sex or low libido

Mental:
- Mental excitement

- Incessant talking and manic behavior
- Impatience without being able to act
- Alternating between laughter and crying without reason

What does the energy of the Triple heater do?

The Triple heater only exists as a meridian, not as an organ. This meridian connects the 'three heaters' in the torso, which are defined in Chinese medicine, through deeper branches.

The lower heater is located between the belly button and the pelvis. The organs in this area (small intestine, large intestine, kidneys, uterus and bladder) take care of excretion and reproduction.

This lower part is the center of our energy. This energy source allows the middle heater to function. This is located between the sternum (breastbone) and the belly button. This area (stomach, spleen, pancreas, Gallbladder and liver) is in charge of digestion. The energy that is released from this, rises like vapor from a pan of boiling soup towards the upper heater: the area between the stomach and the neck. The organs in this area (heart and lungs) are the most pure organs. They are occupied with respiration and circulation of blood and lymphatic fluid. This is where the energy from nutrition connects with that from the air, which creates a form of energy that is suitable for our body. The upper heater distributes this energy throughout all limbs.

So the Triple heater is connected to all other meridians and is in charge of distributing that energy and body heat evenly over the body. The energy of the Triple heater also regulates the hydraulic system of the three different areas of the torso. Besides this the meridian supports our immune system. When you feel cold, you instinctively rub the outside of your arms, where the Triple heater meridian runs. By rubbing you enhance the flow of the meridian, which generates heat, distributes and protects against the cold.

What do you experience when the there is an imbalance in the Triple heater?
An imbalance in this meridian often stems from an overprotective upbringing, or other causes which make a person maladjusted to society or unprepared to face the world. A weak energy in this meridian can present the following symptoms.

Physical:
- Having trouble adjusting to changes in temperature and weather
- Stiff and tense forearms
- Rapid allergic reactions
- Frequent colds and suffering with eyes and nose
- Hearing problems
- Pain in the outer corners of the eyes
- Disorganized thoughts from fatigue
- Sub-luxatation of neck vertebrae, tension in the neck
- Loss of sensation in neck down to the back of the arms
- RSI
- Eyes that have trouble adjusting to the brightness of light

Mental:
- Continuously wary, resulting in tension and rigidity
- Multiple obsessions
- Inability to adapt
- Awkward behavior
- Being overly careful
- Very sensitive
- Defensive attitude

Exercises for the Heart protector and the Triple heater

The following exercises also enhance the energy flow of the Heart protector and the Triple heater.

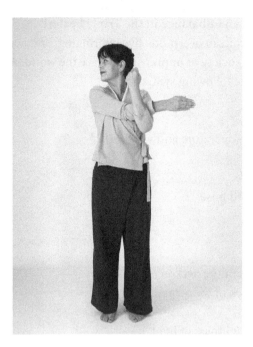

Hook around your arm

Stand with your feet hip-width apart. Place your right arm straight across your chest, the palm of your hand facing backwards. Hook your left arm under and around the right elbow from below. Use your left arm to pull your right arm towards you. Look to the right. This stretches the triple heater in your right shoulder and upper arm and the left side of your neck.

Check if you can experience the improved flow of energy through your shoulder and neck after the exercise.

Pushing walls

For this exercise also start with the feet hip-width apart. Move your arms outwards at shoulder height. Bend your wrists so that your palms face away from you. Maybe you can manage to get your hands vertical. Often the muscles in the forearms are too stiff to achieve this, so don't cross your boundaries. Now push your hands away from you, as if you are positioned between two walls and want to push these away from each other.

Effect: The tingling sensation in your palms is the Heart protector meridian which has been activated by this posture. The stretch relaxes the muscles of the inner arm.

Shielding

Sit in cross-legged position, with your right leg in front. Move the knees as close to the ground as possible. Breathe in, raise your arms up in a circle, cross the right arm behind the left, bend forward and place the crossed hand upon the knees. Without moving the legs, pull the knees towards each other to open the space in between the vertebrae. Relax the neck. Breathe calmly into the lower belly. After a few breaths return to the upright position. Stretch out and bring your arms back down in a circular motion. Now perform this exercise once again in cross-legged position with your left leg in front. This time cross your arms with the left arm behind the right. Effect: This is a relaxing exercise. The forward bend protects all vulnerable (yin) body parts. The tougher and stronger (yang) parts are now facing outwards. This mirrors the function of the Triple heater – which amongst others protects the body from cold – and that of the Heart protector – which protects the energy of the heart from intense emotions. The space in between the shoulderblades is connected to the energy of the Heart and Heart protector.

Rubbing

Rub your hands vigorously but in a relaxed position in front of your chest. This way you are heating up a pressure point on the Heart protector meridian. The name of this point is – *The center of the palm* – which gives the location (also check out the appendix for the exact description of the location). This exercise enhances the flow of energy and blood in your whole body, it calms and supports the health of your heart. It is no coincidence that in many cultures this is regarded as an important *healing* point.

During Korean tea ceremonies one of the first teacups that you use is hold between the palms first, this heats up the hands and activates this same energy point. The idea behind this is, that it will make you feel at ease during the ritual.

Duo arm stretch

This exercise is most effective when performed by two people. Stand with your back against that of your partner. Hook your straight arms behind those of your partner, palms facing forward. During inhalation you both raise your arms so that they are completely stretched upwards. You will experience a stretch along the inside of your arm now, along the pathway of the Heart protector. Bring the arms back down on an exhalation and repeat everything three to five times. After completing this, experience the tingling of energy in your hands.

Intermezzo 5
The cycle of life: the Five transformations

Influencing the flow of energy

In this intermezzo you will be introduced to the Five transformations, a model that explains the natural cycles of life. You will read about how the meridians nourish and control each other and how you can apply the Five transformations to Do-In

Together with the yin and yang model the model of the Five transformations forms the framework of Chinese medicine. For those who wish to properly perform Do-In it is important to know the essence of this framework, because it offers instructions for an effective sequence to the exercises and also gives insight into the effect that the meridians have on each other.

The Five transformations

Over two thousand years ago another model – besides the yin and yang model – emerged in China: the Five transformations, also well-known as the Five phases, the Five elements or Wuxing. This system is based upon the perception that everything in the world develops itself in a cyclic manner: something starts, develops itself, experiences a climax, deteriorates and falls into decay, but from this also forms a new beginning. A tree is an example: a seed falls to the ground, from here a stem and the first leaf develop, after this a tree grows. This tree can live for hundreds of years, but in the end it will eventually deteriorate for example through small animals gnawing away at the trunk, and after this it will die. The material that remains after it expires will form a source of nutrition for new life, which ignites a new cycle.

Such movement is recognizable in almost everything. Take a project into mind, or a human life, but also the course of an illness – a reason why this model is so important in Chinese medicine. Everything comes into existence, grows and blooms, but also deteriorates and decays. The system of the Five transformations however does not put emphasis on the transient nature. It actually shows that everything is always in a state of flux and development. Things do not go to ruin, but they transition into a next phase. *Ki* transforms itself over and over this way.

Natural progression

This perspective was developed by observing nature very closely. That is why each transformation was named after a natural element: Wood, Fire, Earth, Metal and Water. Truly everything can be classified under one of these transformations.

To understand this whole system in a profound way, would take a very long period of study. The next pages therefore focus on the significance of the Five transformations in Do-In. The bibliography in the back of the book lists the titles of books with more specific content pertaining to this subject.

One of the most important associations with the transformations is that of the seasons. This means that Wood represents spring, fire represents summer, earth represents Indian summer, metal represents autumn and water represents winter.

De five phase shen-*cycle: wood is the source of nutrition for fire; the ashes from the fire enrich the earth; earth contains metal; metal is naturally cold which helps water to condense; apart from that metal feeds water because it forms one of its ingredients in the shape of minerals; water is needed to make wood grow.*

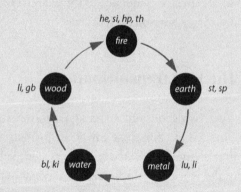

This association shows that the phases have an ideal order; you cannot skip the autumn in a year; within a normal development each phase has its place. This sequence is called the generating cycle, or otherwise known as the shen-cycle

The illustration also shows that each transformation is connected to one or more pairs of meridians and each transformation is associated with different emotions. This

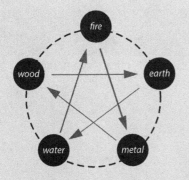

Ko-cycle: the roots of the wood hold the earth together, earth keeps the rivers within their shores, water can extinguish fire, fire will melt metal, metal (an axe) will chop wood.

is important for the therapeutic application of Do-In. A weakened organ can also be strengthened by the meridians that precede it according to the *shen*-cycle. That is why it is useful to not only stretch one part of the body – so just one group of meridians – but in each Do-In class or yoga class to offer exercises for all parts of the body. Especially if this is in an order in which the meridians are connected to each other (according to the Chinese clock, see intermezzo 6) or influence each other.

The different elements can also limit or control each other. This is called the controlling cycle or the *ko*-cycle.

When the different elements are balanced, the nourishing and controlling force will be perfectly equal everywhere. This is what preserves the equilibrium. The image of the Five transformations also shows what happens when everything is imbalanced. In case of a blockage, for example in the Spleen meridian, the Lung meridian in the next phase receives insufficient nutrition. Besides that the controlling cycle shows us that the Earth phase is not strong enough to control the Water, which leads the Water to overflow (become too strong). If this situation persists a dominant Water phase will also affect the Wood element and Fire, etc.

The five phases in Do-In
You can perform Do-In exercises in any order you desire. But do you want the optimum effect from Do-In? Then it is important to follow the sequence of the generating cycle of the different meridians or otherwise the order that will be explained in Intermezzo 6. You can start anywhere in the cycle. After a stretch for Kidney and Bladder (Water), you then chose one for Liver and Gallbladder (Wood), then Heart and Small intestine and Heart protector and Triple heater (Fire), followed by stretches for Stomach and Spleen (Earth) and finally by those for Lung and Large intestine (Metal).

	Wood	Fire
Meridians	Liver and Gall bladder	Heart and Small intestine, Heart protector and Triple heater
Discoloration on the skin when the meridian is imbalanced	Bluish/green	Reddish
Direction of the energy	Outwards, like the branches of a tree	Upward, like fire
State of mind: 1. Balanced; 2. Imbalanced	1. Friendly, creative, assertive, humor. 2. Anger, impatience, edgy, bearing a grudge.	1. Joy, enthusiasm, warm, honest. 2. Hysterical, mental turmoil, cruel.
Mental aspect	Liver: spiritual intelligence, the ego, strategy, planning, sexual energy. Gall bladder: decisiveness.	Heart: awareness, intellect. Small intestine: mental 'digestion'. Heart protector: emotional response. Triple heater: feeling protected.
Season in which this element is extra active	Spring	Summer
Sense in which this element is expressed	Eyes: sight	Tongue: speech
Body parts which express the health of this phase	Ligaments, tendons, joints.	Blood vessels and clear powerful eyes
Weather type that influences the meridians	Wind	Heat
Sound of voice when the phase is imbalanced	Screaming/shrieking	Giggling
Function of the phase within the body	Liver: detoxification. Gall bladder: distribution.	Heart: Emotional and spiritual center. Small intestine: absorption. Heart protector: blood circulation. Triple heater: protection.

This table represents an overview of the associations that belong to the different transformations.

Earth	Metal	Water
Stomach and Spleen	Lung and Large intestine	Kidney and Bladder
Yellowish	White	Black
Circular, like the rotation of earth	Inward, like a magnet	Downwards, water always flows down
1. Sympathetic, open. 2. Overanxious, over empathetic, brooding, gloomy, worried.	1. Optimistic, open, communicative. 2. Sad, depressed, cheerless.	1. Soft, flexible, determined, self assured, brave. 2. Fearful, panicky.
Spleen: memory, thoughts. Stomach: physical and mental stamina, the ability to 'ground'.	Lung: communication. Large intestine: the ability to let go.	Kidney: will power, ambition. Bladder: brain function.
Indian summer and the last eighteen days of each season	Autumn	Winter
Mouth: taste	Nose: sense of smell	Ears: hearing
Flesh and muscles, upper lip (lip not thin or swollen).	Skin and lower lip (lip not thin or swollen).	Bones, hair of the head, eye moisture.
Dampness	Dryness	Cold
Lilting	Weepy	Groaning
Spleen: digestion. Stomach: food intake.	Lung: intake of *ki* from the air. Large intestine: excretion.	Kidney: kinetic energy. Bladder: purification.

You can run through this cycle once or multiple times. You can also use just half a cycle. You can perform the same number of exercises from each pair of meridians, but you can also emphasize a specific pair by using more exercises from that element (transformation). The exercises for Conception vessel and Governing vessel (chapter 7) can be performed after this series or somewhere in-between. The self-massage can also be added on to the meridian stretches at any chosen time.

Because this model is based on natural cycles, it is especially important to not work against the order (you can find two well balanced examples amongst the programs in part 3).

Translated to the body, for example if someone who has a weak Liver meridian and a blocked Kidney meridian (which is not able to nourish the Liver) performs the exercises in the opposite order, this person might feel very uncomfortable after a Liver meridian stretch.

Focus on each separate season
The Five transformations also show us when we could focus on specific meridians. In the spring the natural energies – which we are part of – are in the Wood phase. We can see in the cycle that the Liver and Gallbladder meridians are associated with this. This means that these meridians are extra active in this season, but are also vulnerable. For that reason it is especially good to do a fair amount of exercises that stimulate the Liver and Gallbladder and keep them in motion. You can find examples of this in chapter 6 which covers Liver and Gallbladder. The same goes for the other seasons, but the Earth phase takes a special place in all this. The phase indeed represents the Indian summer – and it is great to give the Stomach and Spleen meridians some extra attention the last eighteen days before Fall starts – but this phase also represents a break between any two other phases. Extra attention for Stomach and Spleen therefore is appropriate during the last eighteen days of each season. This allows the energy to calm down, or in other words 'ground', before the energy of the next season increases.

Putting extra emphasis on a certain transformation can be done by performing a relatively large number of exercises for the chosen meridians. For example when it is Winter, you can choose to perform three or more exercises for Bladder and Kidney after performing a Lung and Large intestine exercise.

6 Distribution of energy, detoxification, flexible joints and fat digestion

Do-In for Liver and Gallbladder

Getting acquainted with the meridians

In this chapter you will read about the location of the energy channels of Liver and Gallbladder, what their function is and which exercises lead to a better flow of these energies. We start off with two exercises that will stimulate the meridians so you are able to experience these energy channels right away.

Stretch for the Liver energy

Seat yourself with your knees on the ground, placing your hips as close to your heels as possible. The insteps of your feet are on the floor. Open your knees as far apart as possible and bend forward with a straight back. Push your sit bones to the back. Place your forehead on the floor and stretch your arms out in front of you. Remain in this position for five to ten calm breaths. In this position you will experience a stretch on the inside of the upper leg, exactly along the pathway of the Liver meridian.

The Liver meridian originates at the big toe (on the lateral side next to the second toe) and runs up along the inner leg, approximately along the line of the inner seam of a pair of trousers. Then it continues along the groin, through the reproductive organs, over the belly towards the ribcage up to about an inch under the nipple. The deeper branch of the Liver meridian runs through the lower belly, upwards along the stomach, liver, Gallbladder and lungs. There is also a part which runs through the throat, around the mouth, through the eye and up to the crown.

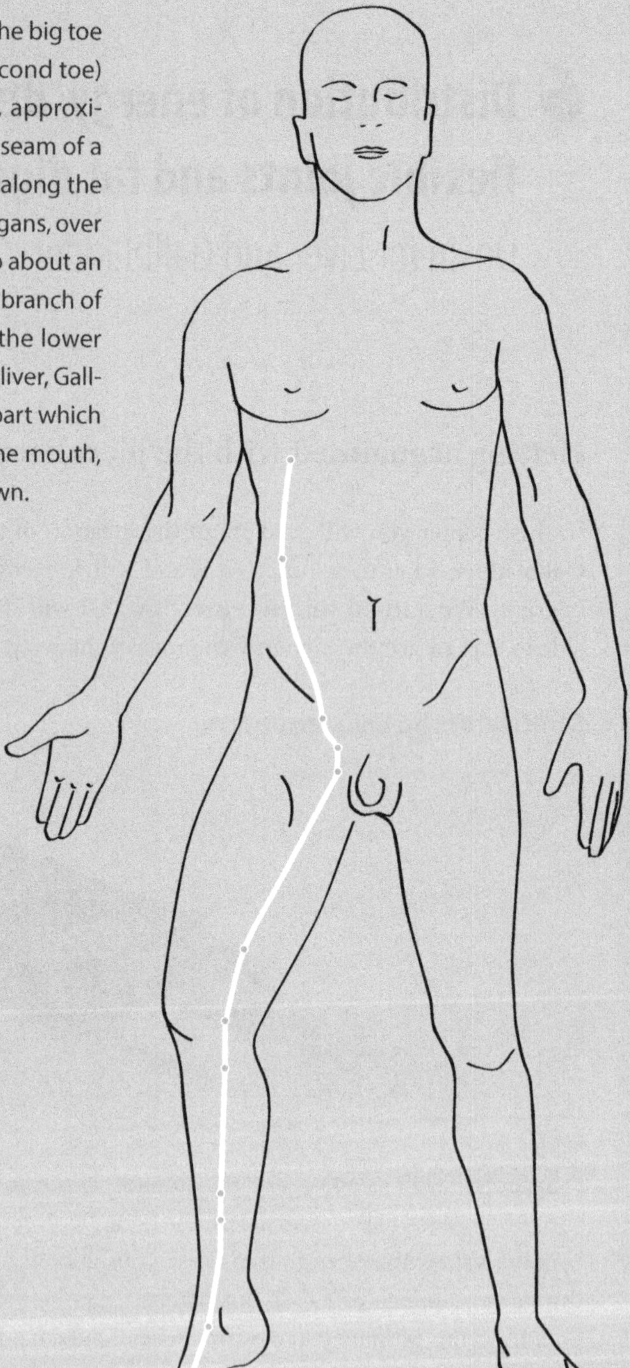

li 3

li 1

The Gallbladder meridian originates at the outer edge of your eyes and then travels a few times back and forth over the side of the head. Then it flows down the side of your neck, along the shoulders, down the ribcage and the outside of your leg (along the outer seam of your trousers) towards the toe next to the pinky toe. The deeper branches of the Gallbladder meridian run along the jaw and connect to the Stomach as well as the Small intestine meridian.

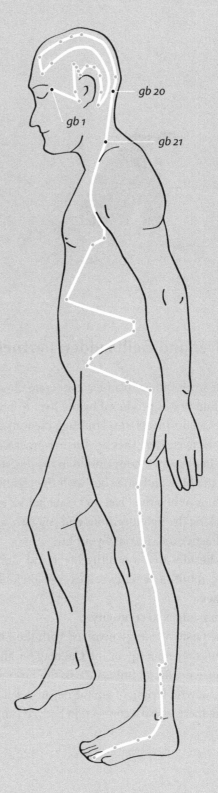

gb 20

gb 1

gb 21

Stretch for the Gallbladder energy

Sit in cross-legged position. Place your left hand next to you on the floor. Carry your right arm up past your ear on an inhale and bend over to the left. Keep both of your sit bones on the floor, while stretching your right arm as far away as possible. Breath in towards the ribs, as if trying to stretch the small muscles between your ribs. Relax your left shoulder down. Stay in this position for five calm breaths, then change sides. In this position you will experience a stretch along the ribcage in the pathway of the Gallbladder meridian.

Liver and Gallbladder: partners

The liver and gallbladder cooperate closely. The gallbladder temporarily stores bile, a fluid that is produced by the liver to break down the fats from our nutrition. These broken down fats travel through the wall of the small intestine, through the portal vein, to the liver. Here they are further processed to be utilized in the body.

Besides their cooperation in the digestive process, their spiritual role is to keep you in the here and now, but with the creativity and imagination to make plans for the future. When the Liver and Gallbladder energy is balanced, you are good at planning, making the right decisions and you have a flexible mind. In this sense these organs also influence the course of your life.

Besides that a healthy Liver and Gallbladder energy is associated with zest for live, intuition, energy, self expression and a need for a harmonious co-existence with others.

From anger to creativity

The positive energy involved with the Liver, is creativity: being able to develop new things. The energy of the Gallbladder allows us to make decisions. The emotion associated with an imbalance in the Liver and Gallbladder, is anger. This also includes discontent, feeling of guilt, a negative self image, frustration and irritation. In our culture there is also a connection between anger and these organs. For example the saying 'having shit on the liver'. Which means you are angry and have something to say that you need to get out (which is indigestible to you). Besides that you might also have heard the Dutch saying 'spewing bile', which means that someone is expressing anger in words or in deeds.

The image of an indigestible incident, shows that the energy has become blocked and is trying to find an alternative way out (spewing). Do-In exercises for the Liver and Gallbladder are helpful, obviously besides expressing your feelings, to neutralize possible anger.

Nutrition for Liver and Gallbladder

Juicy leafy greens and fruit with a slightly sour taste promote the free flow of *ki*. Products that negatively affect this, are: coffee, black tea and very spicy foods. These articles of food disperse the energy briefly and swiftly (the reason why you sweat from spicy foods), but after this it stagnates. Also eating a lot of fatty foods diminishes the energy of the liver.

What does the Liver energy do?

The Liver energy supports the liver organ function. This is how the Liver-*ki* from the meridian assists the liver to produce bile. The Liver energy also supports this organ in its other functions, such as storing blood during times of rest, controlling the blood sugar levels, forming and breaking down proteins and fats, breaking down hormones, digesting and detoxifying foreign body substances such as medications, drugs and alcohol from the body. Besides this the Liver energy nurtures flexible tendons, ligaments and muscles. The condition of the Liver energy also influences all parts of the body which are reached by the deeper branch of the meridian running along the liver, Gallbladder and lungs, through the neck, around the mouth up to the eyes and brain.

A broader function of this energy is making sure that the *ki*, life force energy, is able to flow freely throughout the whole body. When energy can follow its path without stagnation, all physical functions are accommodated and we are also emotionally balanced – for this reason in Chinese medicine the liver is also referred to as 'The seat of the emotions'. The Liver energy affects the whole body.

What do you experience when there is an imbalance in the Liver energy?
The following list is a collection of complaints that regularly occur with a Liver meridian imbalance.

Physical:
- Headache on top or to the side of the head
- Stiff tendons and joints
- Dizziness
- Altered sight or pain in the eyes
- Dull eyes or eyes with a yellow hue
- Hypertension
- Irregular, painful periods
- Pre-menstrual syndrome (among others: painful breasts)
- Emotional asthma, trouble breathing, sore throat
- Experiencing pressure in the right upper quadrant of the belly under the ribs
- Nausea or bloating after eating fatty foods
- Weak sexual activity
- Liver spots
- Broken or ribbed nails

Mental:
- Frustration, depression and sudden bursts of anger
- Bottling up emotions
- Excessive industriousness followed by extreme fatigue
- Tendency to speak with a raised voice
- Having trouble getting started (projects, morning mood, spring fatigue)
- Nervous
- Excessive dreaming, nightmares

What does the Gallbladder energy do?

The Gallbladder energy makes sure the gallbladder is healthy and can perform its duty: producing bile for the digestion. Besides that the spiritual role of the Gallbladder energy is to provide valor. When this energy is balanced, you can properly react to whatever comes your way. The Eastern healing philosophies sometimes describe the Gallbladder energy as the CEO: who takes the decisions and decides on the approach to be taken. If this energy is overly active, this then culminates in an extremely rigid organization, comparable to a company where the CEO exerts too much control over the daily affairs of the employees. When this energy is weak, this can lead to indecision and a lack of activity, just like in a company where the employees have to guess what is expected of them when the CEO never gives direction to the purpose of the work.

What do you experience when there is an imbalance in the Gallbladder energy?
Complaints that present themselves along the pathway of a meridian, such as for example eczema, usually have to do with the associated meridian.

When there is a problem with the Gallbladder meridian the following symptoms may also arise.

Physical:
- Tense jaws
- Gall stones
- Stiff joints (shoulders, ribs, hips, knees, etc.)
- Nausea, vomiting, bitter/sour taste in the mouth
- Jaundiced eyes or skin
- Pain in the eyes and/or the ears
- Headache in the temples
- Gall stone episodes, acid reflux or stomach cramps
- Deficiency of bile, having trouble digesting food
- Dizziness

Mental:
- Anger and rash decisions
- Over-planning and thinking (resulting in insomnia)
- Being timid and lacking initiative
- Too many responsibilities: busy, busy, busy
- Indecisiveness and shyness
- The tendency to suppress things

Exercises for balancing Liver and Gallbladder energy

The next few exercises also enhance the flow of Liver and Gallbladder meridian energy.

This selection is meant to give you an idea which type of postures stimulate these meridians. Do you know any other postures that let you experience a stretch in these areas? Feel free to combine them with this series, they are all beneficial to the Liver and Gallbladder.

Lubricating the joints

Position yourself on hands and knees. Place the hands directly under your shoulders, your knees directly under your hips. Dig your toes into the ground. Make circular movements with your upper body; your hands and legs remain where they are. Repeat this for at least a minute (turn right and left circles). If the wrists or hands hurt you can still perform this exercise. In that case just make smaller circles, so that there is less pressure on the wrists. Effect: This exercise simultaneously relaxes all the major joints (shoulders, hips, knees, wrists, back), in such a way that you support the Liver meridian – which actually lubricates the joints – in its task.

Fan

Start out sitting on the ground, with your legs stretched out in front of you. Bend your right leg, move the foot to the left and thus place your right lower leg in front of you. Also bend the left leg with the foot facing left, and place your left leg next to your left with the knee facing forward. Bring your right hand behind you and your left hand onto your right knee. On the inhalation extend through your back, stretching your crown to the ceiling. On the next exhalation turn to the right, sitting on your right buttock. Stay here for five to ten full breaths.

Then rotate back. You are leaning on your right hand which is next to you. Your left hand swings through a half circle in front of you and you extend your arm diagonally up. In this position you stretch from your knee to the tips of your fingers.

Effect: both exercises stretch the Gallbladder meridian along the side of your ribs and leg. This strengthens the energy of the Gallbladder, creates more space for the breath, softens the spine and relaxes the hips. The first variation where you twist the stomach, also stimulates the elimination of toxins.

Duo-side-stretch

The next exercises can also be performed solo. The bonus of working as a duo is that you support each other in stretching further.

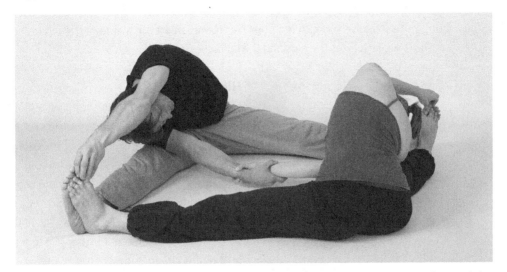

Sit across from each other with spread legs. Let your feet touch each other. If one of the partners has a less wide posture, then he/she can place the feet against the ankles or lower legs of the other. Let the toes point upwards. Take each other's right hand. Extend the spinal column towards the crown and feel your sit bones against the ground. Now each bend sideways with a straight back, in such a way that your right flank moves towards the right upper leg. Stretch the left arm over your head and point the left hand towards the right foot. Body and face remain faced forwards, so your sides are stretched and your chest can open itself. This provides more space for breathing. Send your breath to the ribs on your left side. Return to an upright position after five to ten full breaths and change sides. The Gallbladder meridian runs along the line of tension in your side, the Liver meridian runs along the line of tension on the inner legs.

Now take hold of both of your partners hands or forearms. One hangs back whilst pulling the other forward. After a few breaths you return to upright position and the other hangs back. You can move back and forth a few times. Or move in cicles.

Effect: During this exercise you can feel the Liver meridian on the inside of the leg being stretched. The exercise relaxes the hips and the inner legs.

Hip opener

Lie on your back. Bring the right knee half way up to your chest and place your left ankle over your right knee. Grab hold of your right thigh. Push your left knee away from you. At the same time your arms bring your right knee towards your chest. Imagine using strength from your *hara* to achieve this. This will help you to relax your shoulders. After five to ten full breaths change sides.

Effect: This stretch enhances the flow of the Gallbladder meridian along your hip, which helps to relax the hip.

Beware: during this exercise pressure is exerted on the muscles of the pelvic floor. During pregnancy this exercise is to be performed less deeply or not at all.

Acu-point

Between the metatarsals of your big toe and the second toe, about one centimeter (just under a half inch) above the knuckle of the big toe, a very important acu-point is located. This is the third point (*tsubo*) on the Liver meridian. Light pressure here (just hard enough that it is still pleasant) helps to dissolve energy stagnations. Almost any type of pain and tension is a stagnation, so you can treat this point at many different moments, for example when you experience a headache. In that case press on this point from one to five minutes on each foot.

Beware: do not treat this *tsubo* during pregnancy, because this could also induce labor.

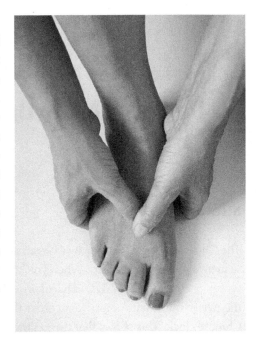

Dandelion leaf salad for detoxification

In cases of spring fatigue, or other signs that your Liver energy is weak, it can be useful to cleanse your liver. For example by eating lots of refreshing, green vegetables and fruits (products that are readily available in spring) and drinking nettle tea. For added effect you can garnish your salads with little dandelion leafs, a plant with a bitter taste that grows almost everywhere. Pick the undamaged leafs without discoloration, which are not larger than 2 inches (discoloration could be a clue that a dog might have urinated over the leafs). Don't pick plants close to roads.

To support the intestines in eliminating the toxins from your liver, you can treat your abdomen daily by massaging it in a circular motion following the direction of the intestines: start at your right hip, then continue along under the right ribs (over the liver) to the left and then descend to your left hip. Massage your abdomen in this fashion for five minutes.

Intermezzo 6
Do-In and biorhythms: the Chinese clock

Stimulating harmony

The Chinese clock, also known as Organ clock is also a model that can be a guide for the sequence of Do-In exercises. When you stick to this order, you will stimulate the natural flow of energy in your body and harmonise your biorhythms. The *ki* as such flows through the twelve meridians in a specific order throughout the day. This order is shown in the Chinese clock. This shows that the *ki* flows through the yin and yang meridians by how they are connected to each other. These meridians also each belong to the same phase. The difference between the Chinese clock and the model of the five phases is that the five phases show how the meridians *influence each other*, whereas the Chinese clock shows in which order the meridians *flow through the body*. Both systems provide an optimum effect of the exercises, they harmonize the movements in the body to that of our natural environment.

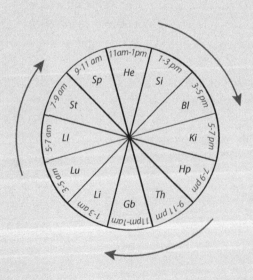

The Chinese clock also shows that each meridian has a specific time of day where it is most active. Mostly these periods are at a logical moment. When you want to strengthen a specific meridian – for example when you regularly experience an energy dip at a certain hour of the day – you can perform Do-In for that meridian at the time that it is most active according to the Chinese clock. When you wake up at night regularly at a particular moment, you could stretch the meridians concerned (often Liver) before you go to bed.

Active periods per meridian

The Lung meridian is most active between **3 am and 5 am**. Our body absorbs more oxygen during this period to acquire energy for the whole day. According to Chinese medicine this is the most optimal time to rise and start the day with Do-In, Tai Chi or Qi Gong.

From **5 am to 7 am** the Large intestine meridian is most active. After performing physical exercises the bowel has been activated by the deep breathing and movements. This is why it is the optimal time for a bowel movement to empty out and start the new day afresh.

The Stomach meridian is most active between **7 am and 9 am**, the time of our breakfast. It is not for nothing that people say breakfast is the most important meal of the day. We can acquire the most energy from it, because the stomach has the most energy available for digestion at this time.

From **9 am to 11 am** the Spleen meridian follows, which according to Chinese medicine plays an important role in digestion, so we are able to digest breakfast well. The most pure ingredients from the breakfast have then already reached the blood.

From **11 am to 1 pm** the Heart meridian is most active. This connects the purest nutritional elements with the *ki* from the air, so we can produce our own *ki* from this. The period between 11 am and 1 pm is seen as the period with the most energy and activity: the sun is at its highest point and delivers the most warmth. The Heart meridian, which belongs to the fire element, is the most yang of the yin-meridians and makes sure that at the time of day where energy is most abundant, we also have drawn the greatest amount of energy from our food. This is also a perfect moment of the day to spend with others: spend you lunchtime with friends or nice collegues, have fun and strenghten your Heart energy.

The Small intestine meridian is most active between **1 pm and 3 pm**. Our breakfast has now reached this part of the digestive tract, providing opportunity for the small intestine to filter out the remaining nutrients.

Then the Bladder meridian follows from **3 pm to 5 pm**. According to Chinese medicine there is a close connection between small intestine and the Bladder meridian. Thanks to this connection it is possible for the bladder to acquire fluids to eliminate waste products. It's important to drink enough at this time of the day.

The Kidney meridian has its active period from **5 pm to 7 pm**. The waste products that have made their way into our bloodstream during the day can now be filtered out most efficiently.

Then the Heart protector and Triple heater meridians follow from **7 pm to 11 pm**. This is the time where the (emotional) impressions that we have accumulated during the day, are discussed with others or filed away appropriately one way or another.

Between **11 pm and 3 am** the Gallbladder and Liver meridians are most active, they take care of purifying our body during our sleep. This allows us to start a new day all refreshed.

Logical order

The sequence in the Chinese clock seems logical when you view the location of the meridians: the Lung meridian ends on the thumb. This is right next to the Large intestine
meridian, which starts on the index finger. After the Lung meridian the Large intestine
meridian is most active. The end of the Large intestine meridian is under the nostril; an
inch away on the cheek the first *tsubo* of the Stomach meridian is located. In this sense
the network of meridians forms a free flowing entirety.

The Chinese clock and Do-In

When you want to work according to the Chinese clock, you basically can start at ran-
dom with any organ. Often the Lung meridian is the starting point, because this is so
closely related to life itself – just think of the first breath of a baby, and it's connection
to the start of a new day. After the Lung meridian, or in essence the transformation of
metal, you can follow the Chinese clock as a further guideline.

Two of the meridians, which are also addressed in this book, Conception vessel and
Governing vessel are neither represented in the Chinese clock nor in the Five transformations. These meridians belong to the 'extraordinary' meridians and they follow a
different cycle in the body. The exercises for Conception vessel and Governing vessel
can be performed before or after the series according to the Five transformations or
the Chinese clock. Another good moment is after the stretches for the Bladder and
Kidney meridian.

Meridians and elements

Organ	Element
Lung and large intestine	Metal
Spleen, pancreas and stomach	Earth
Heart and small intestine	Fire
Kidney and bladder	Water
Heart protector and triple heater	Fire
Liver and gallbladder	Wood

You can read more about the elements in intermezzo 5:
The cycle of life: the Five transformations.

7 Activity, rest and energy
Do-In for the Conception vessel and the Governing vessel

Getting acquainted with the meridians

In this chapter you will read about the pathway of the most important yin and yang meridian and which exercises promote the flow in these energy channels. We start off with two exercises that will stimulate the meridians so you are able to experience these energy channels right away.

Stretch for the Conception vessel

Start out in prone position. Bend your legs and grab your insteps. If you cannot reach your feet you can hold onto your pant legs, or wrap a shawl around your ankles and hold on to this. To stretch the Conception vessel, lift your legs and torso up as high as you can on each inhalation. Push out the feet upwards and backwards. Also lift your pelvic floor (the sensation of having to pee, but holding it in) to protect your lower back.

You can feel a stretch in your chest and abdomen. Relax on each exhalation. Try to hold your knees as close together as possible when you lift your legs.

This exercise is not suitable during periods (menstruation) and pregnancy, and also be careful while performing this if you suffer from back problems. After this exercise you round out your back as far as you can for a few moments, as a countermovement for the arched position. A wonderful and relaxing exercise for example would be child's pose: sitting on your knees you bring your buttocks towards your heels and you bend forwards to lean your head on the ground, relax here for a while.

The Conception vessel (also known under the Chinese name *ren mai*) originates in the middle of the belly at the 'moving energy be-tween the kidneys', the energetic center in the lower belly, the *hara*. The meridian surfaces between the anus and the sexual organs and proceeds along the front of our body at the midline towards the chin. An internal branch circles the mouth and ends under the eyes, on the first point of the Stomach meridian. There also is an internal branch that runs to the arm.

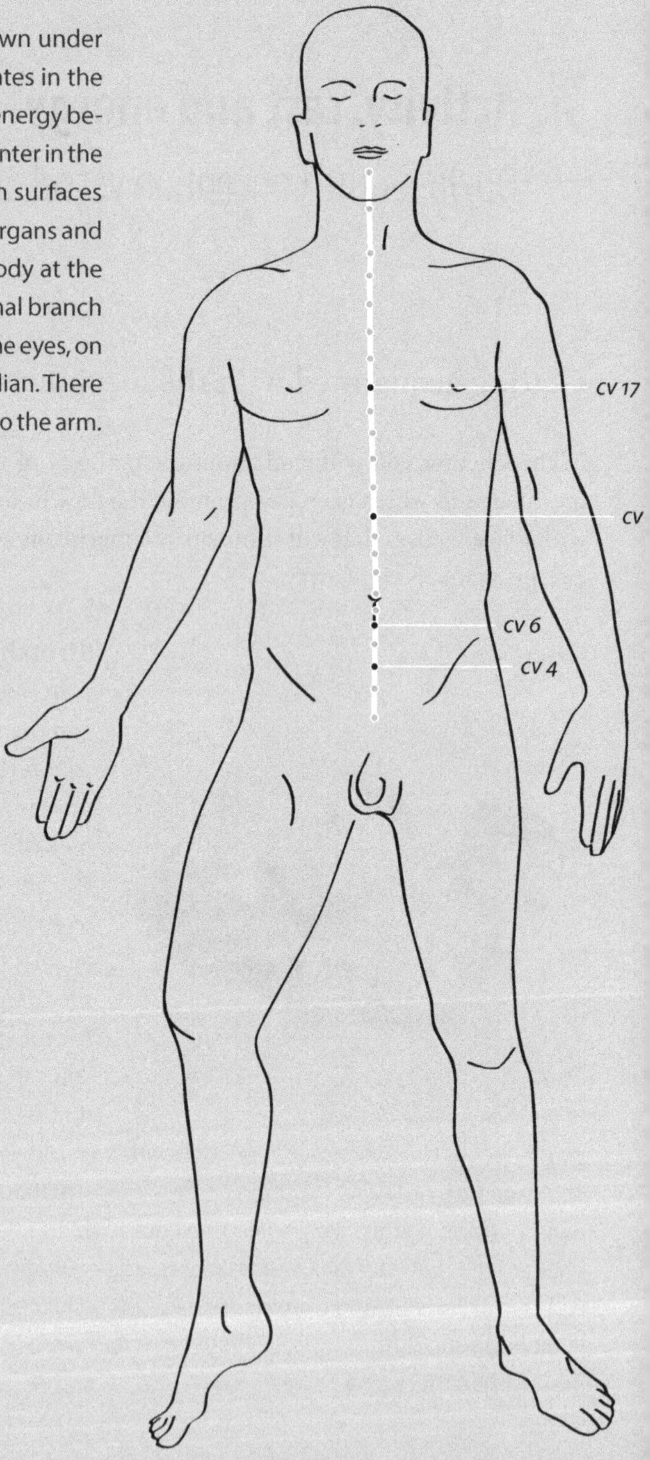

CV 17

CV

CV 6

CV 4

The Governing vessel (also known as *du mai*) originates, similarly to the Conception vessel, in the center of our body. After this it descends and surfaces between the anus and the sexual organs. It runs upward along the spinal column over the head to the upper teeth.

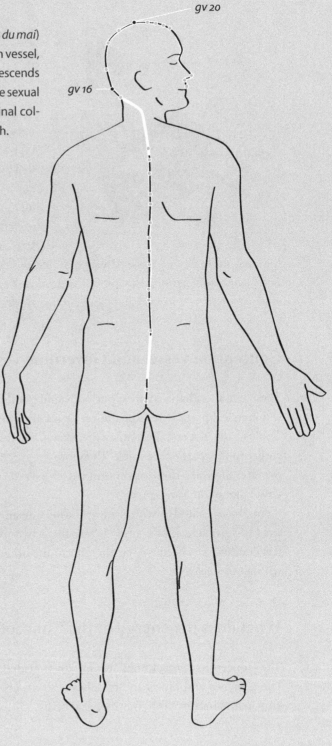

gv 20

gv 16

Stretch for the Governing vessel

Lay down in supine position. Grab onto the soles of your feet or your knees and softly roll back and forth from the lower back to the area between the shoulder blades. Round out your back as much as possible so all of the vertebrae are massaged against the ground. Feel that the power to roll originates from the hara. Roll back and forth ten times. Build this up to fifty times each morning and evening. This exercise stimulates the Governing vessel. This strengthens the back and kidneys, nourishes the brain and bone marrow and clears the mind. Besides that this back roll provides you with energy when you perform it in the morning. And in the evening it ensures that the stagnated energy from your head, neck and shoulders flows further, which helps your mind to calm itself.

Conception vessel and Governing vessel: partners

These two meridians encircle our body and divide it in two – seen from the outside – symmetrical parts. The Conception vessel and the Governing vessel are, just like the Triple heater, not so called 'organ meridians', like the other meridians which are covered earlier in this part of the book. Therefore they are not named after organs, but play an overarching role. The Conception vessel governs the yin-energy and the Governing vessel that of the yang-energy.

In Do-In, but also within other Eastern healing disciplines, these meridians are used to solve a lack of energy. When these two meridians become free flowing, you feel comfortable, because the energies of the other meridians can perform their duty without obstacles.

What does the energy of the Conception vessel do?

The Conception vessel regulates all yin-meridians (Heart, Heart protector, Spleen. Lung, Kidney and Liver) and circulates the yin-energy through the body. This yin-energy maintains our body, our material being.

The name Conception vessel in itself suggests that this meridian is also connected to reproduction and fertilization (conception). It nourishes the reproductive organs – primarily the uterus – and regulates the menstrual cycle.

What do you experience with imbalance?
A stagnation in the Conception vessel expresses itself in various complaints in the abdominal region, the reproductive organs and in the flow of fluids in the body. Also in Eastern medicine chronic diseases are treated through this meridian.

Physical:
- Early aging
- Diminishing appetite
- Stomach and abdominal pain
- Respiratory diseases
- Troubled digestion in stomach and intestines
- Irregular periods (menstruation)
- Cysts
- Abundant white discharge (in women)
- Problems during pregnancy
- Hemorrhoids
- Heart problems
- Pain in bones
- Pain in lumbar region (low back)
- Afflictions of the nervous system
- Problems in the urinary tract (urine incontinence or retention)
- Hot flashes
- Edema

Mental:
- Finding it hard to take on responsibilities
- Demonstration of autocratic behavior
- Demonstration of exaggerated social behavior
- Having no sense of one's surroundings
- Lack of love for oneself

What does the energy of the Governing vessel do?

The Governing vessel regulates the yang-meridians (Small intestine, Triple heater, Stomach, Large intestine, Bladder and Gallbladder). The power of the Governing vessel can be measured from the constitution of the back. Is this straight and flexible? Then the meridian has unobstructed flow. This means that we are active and enterprising, enjoy clear thought processes and have a strong memory and intellect.

What do you experience when there is an imbalance in this energy?
The Governing vessel runs right through the spinal column and therefore is a major influence on our back and nervous system. Most physical complaints connected to an imbalance will present themselves along the pathway of this meridian.

Physical:
- Distortion of the spinal column
- Pain in the back or painful areas on the back
- Weak back
- Weakening of muscles and organs
- Pain in the neck
- Trouble with the joints, feeling tight
- Headache
- Sensitivity to colds and flu
- Perspiring easily and getting cold swiftly
- Cold and/or loss of sensation in the hands and feet
- Bowing the head in important conversations
- Epilepsy
- Dementia
- Blood in stools
- Unwanted loss of urine
- Painful urination
- Irregular periods (menstruation)
- Infertility
- Dry throat
- Dizziness
- Ringing of the ear (tinnitus)
- Fever

Mental:
- Weak and compliant
- Feeling washed out
- Having too many thoughts to be able to sleep
- Lack of concentration
- Short memory
- Depressed
- Extremely extravert or on the contrary afraid to explore the world

Exercises for the Conception vessel and the Governing vessel

The pathways of the Conception vessel and the Governing vessel together form a circle around the abdomen and the back known as microcosmic orbit. Most of the exercises that alternate between arching and rounding the back therefore stimulate these meridians. Exercises for these meridians help the Lungs to bring down *ki* from the air, so the Kidneys can receive this. This allows you to breathe more freely and to derive more energy from each breath.

Cat

Position yourself on hands and knees. Place your hands directly under your shoulders and your knees right under your hips. Arch your back on an inhale and round it on an exhale. This exercise alternately opens the Conception vessel and the Governing vessel. When you contract your belly button actively during the exhalation, you will feel warmth arising from the lower belly. Relax your belling during inhalation. Repeat at least ten times.
Effect: This is a wonderful way to warm up and to make the back more flexible.

Bending

Stand up straight. Lift your arms while inhaling, look up and arch the back slightly. Swing the arms to the front, down and back up and forward again while exhaling. At the same time you incorporate bending of the knees in this movement. On the next inhale you raise your arms again. Repeat twenty times and feel the energy flowing through your body after this.

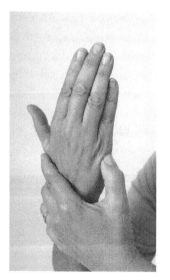

Acu-point Governing vessel

To find this *tsubo* look at the palm of your hand and locate the top of three large lines on your hand. This line continues to the edge of the hand under the pinky finger. If you wiggle it around a bit or move your thumb in a circular motion there, you will end up in a small dent. This is the third point of the Small intestine meridian, but this point also regulates the flow of energy through the Governing vessel. It is used to strengthen the energy in cases of exhaustion. Press on this line with the thumb of your other hand, right under the joint of the pinky finger. Apply light pressure for at least one minute, or use a circular motion. Treat the point on the other hand as well. Effect: This *tsubo* is used to strengthen the back and to clear the mind.

Acu-point Conception vessel

This *tsubo* is located on the inside of the arm, two thumb widths under the crease of the wrist on the side of the thumb. You can perceive a slight dent in the bone there. This is the seventh point on the Lung meridian. Apart from strengthening the Lung energy, pressure on this *tsubo* benefits sufficient flow through the Conception vessel. Apply light pressure or

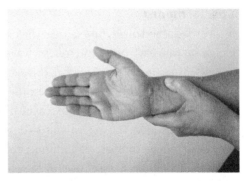

use a circular motion on this point for at least one minute. Then treat the other wrist.

Use this point in cases of headaches, a stiff neck or a weak memory. Besides that, this point enhances the cooperation between the middle and upper heater (read more about the heaters in chapter 5), which allows you to produce more *ki* (you are able to connect the energy from nutrition to that from the air) and feel more energetic. This pressure point also improves the flow through the meridians by dispersing accumulation of fluids.

Breathing exercise for more energy

Start out in cross-legged position or in *seiza*. Line up the fingers of one hand on the lower belly right under your belly button. Lightly press the fingers into the belly on the exhalation. Breathe in so deeply that your fingers are pushed out by the breath (and not by the muscle tension!). Repeat this for 5 minutes. If this area is sensitive, you can also place your palm over your lower abdomen and breathe towards your hand.

Even though this exercise sounds simple, for some people it is initially quite difficult. It just seems impossible for them to breathe down into the lower belly. If you also find this is dif-

ficult, then don't give up. Repeat this exercise daily for a few weeks, and you will find that it will become more natural for you to breathe deeper. It will probably also provide you with more energy. The fingertips on the lower abdomen after all are stimulating the famous *ki kai* point, which is positioned on the Conception vessel. This point is a powerful source of energy. You can read more about the effect of proper breathing in chapter 2 of part 2.

Special *mudra*

A very special and powerful exercise which connects the Conception vessel and the Governing vessel with each other and sends a wave of *ki* through it, is *kan ro* (also known under the name *kichi mudra* or *kechari mudra*). This exercise has been passed on from teacher to student for centuries and creates inner balance. The mental peace that this *mudra* offers, is a perfect departure point for meditation. Of maybe it would be better to say that this mental calm and clarity is meditation. This *mudra* is also – due to its strong balancing force – recommended to people suffering from cancer to support their recovery process.

This exercise is built up out of several stages. The first two can be performed by anyone during the total practice of Do-In. Especially the fourth stage takes several months or maybe years of practice to master for most people.

Step 1

Place the tip of your tongue against your palate, right behind your two front teeth. Concentrate on the sensations that you experience for five minutes.

Most people experience a slight tingling sensation on the tongue within a minute. The saliva becomes more liquid, and there is more saliva in the mouth – both improve the digestion. Also the taste of the saliva can alter. Besides that it is possible to feel the area of the kidneys heat up, because you are balancing the yin and yang energies with each other. The energy of the Kidneys is often depleted from an over-active lifestyle and too much turmoil in our head. When yin and yang are balanced by the connection between the Conception vessel and the Governing vessel, the kidneys become more energized, which is perceived as warmth. Another effect of this exercise is a sensation of calm, a sense of grounding, or the perception that you can view everything around yourself from a distance. The respiration can also feel calmer or deeper.

Step 2

Fold the tongue in half with the tip towards the throat. The bottom of the tongue now fits nicely into the curve of the palate. Once again concentrate for five minutes on the sensations in the mouth and the rest of the body.

This stretch along the bottom of the tongue stretches the Kidney meridian, which has internal branches along the veins that run under the tongue to the tip of the tongue. Besides that the tip of the tongue is connected to the Heart energy. This stretch further balances the elements Water and Fire more deeply in the body, which you can feel amongst others as a sensation of tingling or energy in the heart region. Breathing becomes easier. Moreover this stretch offers more trust and a sense of peace and completeness.

Step 3

The third level of kan-ro will be challenging to some at first, but practice makes perfect! Bring the tip of the tongue further back to the soft palate at the root of the uvula. Keep the tongue in this position for five minutes and concentrate on the changes that this brings to your body.

This exercise offers a sense of peace. Fearful thoughts or a sense of rushed agitation subside. The stretch on the back of the tongue offers assistance in solving stagnations in the energy of the kidneys. These stagnations can be caused by, or are the root of fears – the reason why these feelings subside through this exercise.

If you can hold this position for a longer period, say for example 45 minutes during a meditation, then you can experience the sixth chakra (*ajna*), also called the third eye (the space just above the middle of the eyebrows) opening up. This might feel like a light pressure, or like this spot is moving slightly forward. The process of opening up strengthens your intuition and stimulates the pituitary gland as well as the pineal gland. These are two glands in the brain that amongst other things produce hormones for the growth of bones and muscles, which support the effect of the thyroid, promote the maturation of cells in the reproductive organs, just to name a few of the effects. The pituitary gland also produces endorphins that are analgesic, but also offer a sensation of euphoria and ecstasy.

Step 4

This last step is almost never taken by anyone in just one go. It is a step which only people who persist will complete eventually, after several months (or more) of practice. Remember not to push yourself, enjoy the practice.

In this fourth step the tongue travels back even further, past the uvula. The tongue is hereby placed in the opening behind the bridge of the nose and touches the skin directly under the pituitary gland. The sensation that is felt in this final stage, is similar to breathing liquid white light. The taste sensation is sweet and therefore this exercise is also called 'tasting the heavenly nectar'. When you achieve this, your perception alters and your consciousness is raised. It's very likely you notice these effects in earlier stages as well. Respiration deepens, the amount of phlegm in the body diminishes, the circulation of *ki* and blood improves, emotional disturbances decrease, which offers more mental balance. Yogi's who go off to meditate for months on end in the mountains, often use this *mudra* because the heavenly nectar and the balance that this brings to the body, provides much less need for food and drink.

But how do you get that tongue so far back into the throat? There are several exercises you can use to achieve that.

- Stick out your tongue as far as possible and try to touch the tip of your nose and chin with it.
- Stick out your tongue, hold it with your fingers and pull the tongue out and then swiftly but softly move the tongue back and forth.
- Move the tongue back towards the uvula. Place your fingertips on the bottom of your tongue and help yourself to move further this way.

It might take a good long while before your tongue is resting comfortably in the nasal cavity. The positive effects of this exercise start to grow as soon as you experience a sensation of comfort and relaxation.

Part 2
Other aspects of Do-In: self-massage, breathing and meditation

Apart from the meridian stretches that were mentioned in the preceding chapters, Do-In also is comprised of three other important disciplines: self-massage, breathing techniques and meditative practice. Combined together they transform this philosophy of movement into a comprehensive system to stay healthy and young or to become more healthy. Exactly like the meridian stretches these exercises have been transferred from teacher to student – due to their healing properties – through thousands of years.

These exercises teach you to control the *ki* of the body. Using the self-massage you can unblock stagnation in the meridians. Through the breathing exercises you will be able to gather *ki* from the air and make it descend into the lower belly, providing you with more energy. Meditation allows *ki* to be gathered into the *hara*, the center, which provides energy, realization and power.

Maybe you don't have time every day to perform the meridian stretches, self-massage, breathing exercises and meditations. But the advantage of the exercises from this chapter is that you can almost perform them everywhere and always. When you apply day or night crème to your face, you might just as well simultaneously massage the skin according to the Taoist method. When you are travelling on a train there is more than enough room to massage your fingers and hands. And in the evening on the couch or in bed, you can pull up a foot and treat it. While you are waiting in the check-out line, you can bring your attention to your breath. And a meditation can easily be done while you walk.

Which ways are there to integrate Do-In into your daily life? Could you add more vegetables of the season? Might you just stretch a little longer when picking up a book from the highest shelf (and maybe stretch your other side as well)? Could you open your window in the morning with a slow yet big swing of your arm to open the Lung meridian, and take a deep breath? Or take an extra moment to massage your skull while washing your hair? All these simple and small changes to your daily life, benefit the flow of ki and enlarge your self healing capacity.

1 Self shiatsu

Massage to improve the flow of energy

Rejuvenating techniques

Self-massage, whether we are talking about your face, feet, hands or belly, has an enormous effect on the flow of energy in the whole body. The meridians all originate at the tips of the fingers and toes and connect with each other through internal branches. It is very possible that your headache will disappear when you treat your feet. Or you can experience more relaxation throughout your whole body after a facial massage. During your practice of Do-In it is the most obvious choice to start or to end with the self-massage.

These self-massages, sometimes also referred to as self acupressure, are all considered rejuvenating techniques. Wrinkles for example will not occur as soon because the skin is nourished with life force, and more relaxed with improved circulation, which helps to eliminate toxins more effectively. This does not only apply to the face, but for example also for hands and feet. More information on the healing properties of the exercises is included in the descriptions below.

Preparation

Make sure that your hands are warm when you start the self-massage. If you want to heat up your hands quickly, then rub the palms together. Simultaneously lift your pelvic floor – you can do this by tensing the same muscles that you use when you need to urinate, but have to hold off. Also press the tip of your tongue against your palate. Visualise the *ki* flowing towards the hands. This way the hands will warm up with *ki*.

Basic massage for the whole body

After this exercise all your limbs will slightly tingle from improved circulation. This allows subcutaneous waste products to be eliminated away more effectively and the muscles will subsequently relax. That is especially wonderful if you have a stiff neck and a back ache!

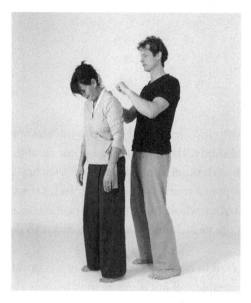

Basic position: Stand with your feet hip-width apart. The toes point straight forward and the knees are straight but loose. Now close the hands into a relaxed fist.

Head and neck – start to tap on the head with the relaxed fists. Keep the fists close to each other and travel around your head: the front hairline, the top, the back, the sides and the edge of the skull. Drop down to the neck and tap the side and back of the neck.

Upper back – Ask someone else to tap on your upper back. This is one area you won't be able to reach yourself! Hang forward slightly while the other person taps all over the back.

Shoulders and arms – Let your right hand tap on the muscles near the left shoulder – don't tap on your shoulder (the acupressure point Gallbladder 21, see appendix) in case of pregnancy. Then run over the pathway of the meridians in the left arm a few times. While doing this you follow the direction of flow in the meridians. Tap from the shoulder down the inside of the arm to the thumb; this is the Lung meridian. Then return from the index finger on the outside of the arm back to the shoulder; the Large intestine meridian. Subsequently tap the inside of the arm down to the middle finger along the Heart protector meridian.

And back up along the Triple heater: starting at the ring finger tapping along the midline of the outer arm. Finally tap the inside of the arm to the pinky finger – Heart meridian – and up along the back outside of the arm; Small intestine meridian. By tapping your arm this way, all of the meridians in this part of the body will experience improved flow.

Also perform the exercise on the other arm.

You can find more information about the meridians in part 1 of this book.

Chest – tap the chest next to the insert of the shoulder joint, just under the clavicle. This is where important acu-points, *tsubo's*, for the lungs are located. Tap the side of the ribcage and then down over the sternum (breastbone). Relaxed chest muscles can literally give you a sense of relief. Moreover this can also help alleviate pain in the upper back, which is often linked to a great deal of tension in the upper thorax.

 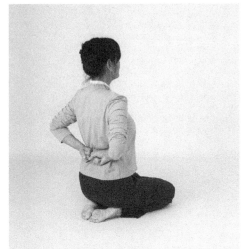

Abdomen – start near the right hip. Then calmly tap up towards the area just under the right ribs. Tap along the edge of the ribs to the area under the left ribs. Descend down to the left hip. Then travel over to the right hip, creating a number of circles this way over the abdomen. It is important to tap in this direction, because this is the direction that the large intestine flows in. This stimulates the release of toxins.

Lower back and hips – start tapping as high up as you can on your lower back. And then descend to the sacrum and the buttocks, then tap on the hips and the front next to both sides of the pubic bone.

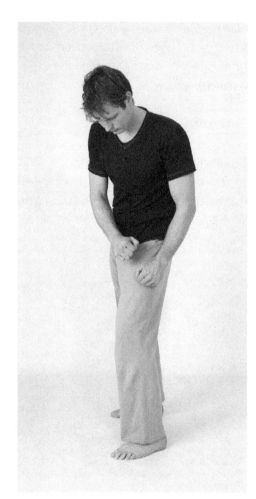

Legs – just like with the arms, we tap on the legs according to the direction of flow of the meridians. The yangmeridians flow down to the toes. The yin-meridians flow up from the toes. Start on the front of the thigh, along the outside of the knee down to the foot, this is the Stomach meridian. Then tap along the inside of the shin and the knee back up to the groin along the Spleen meridian. Subsequently follow the Gallbladder meridian along the outside of the leg down to the top of the foot and come back up along the Liver meridian on the inside of the leg. Finally tap along the Bladder meridian on the back of the leg going down and follow the Kidney meridian up again, which is situated right behind the Liver meridian, on the inside back of the leg. This will allow all the meridians in your legs to experience improved flow. More information on the meridians can be found in part 1 of this book.

After this exercise, close your eyes and feel the current sensations in your body.

Bean bag

Remember the bean bags that you used to throw over cans with at the carnival? Bags like that are really nice to use for tapping on the meridians. They are easy to make yourself from old bits of fabric. You can fill the bags with dried mung beans, little green dried beans which you can buy at Oriental markets and natural health food stores. They stimulate releasing toxins and excessive heat from our body.

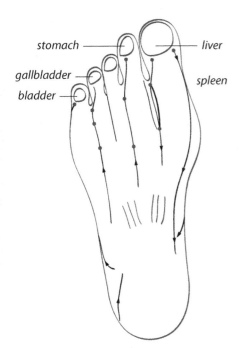

stomach — liver
gallbladder
bladder — spleen

Foot massage

A foot massage is very relaxing and influences all organs. This technique is particularly recommended at times you are very busy, when you have a headache or when you have cold feet.

The hands and feet are the first areas where we age: toes warp, the skin of the hands becomes dehydrated, veins harden and we see liver spots emerging. These are the areas that get cold first due to declining circulation. To warm up, it is therefore important to warm up the feet and hands first. This improves the flow of energy in all meridians, which makes you warm up faster. This improved circulation prevents these body parts from aging.

Ankles – Sit comfortably with a straight back. Pull up one foot. Grab the ankle with one hand and the toes with the other. Make circles with the foot to loosen up the ankle.

Sole of the foot – Now rub the tips of the thumbs along the sole of the foot towards the toes, not just along the midline, but also towards the edges. Apply mild pressure during the rubbing. Then tap the fist on the sole of the foot. The tapping technique is the same as with the *Basic massage for the whole body*.

Instep – Slide your fingers along the instep a few times between the metatarsals from the toes up to the ankles. Pay special attention the sensitive spots in the grooves between the metatarsals. During pregnancy please skip the groove behind the big and second toe. The *tsubo's* that are located here, will unblock stagnation of energy, which will reduce pain, but can possibly induce labor.

Toes – grab your big toe with one hand. With your free hand you can hold on to the ball of your foot to support the joints during the toe massage. While you pull to slightly extend the toe, you make circles with it in both directions. This keeps the joint flexible. Following this, stretch the toe forwards to the instep as far as possible a few times as well as back down towards the sole of the foot.

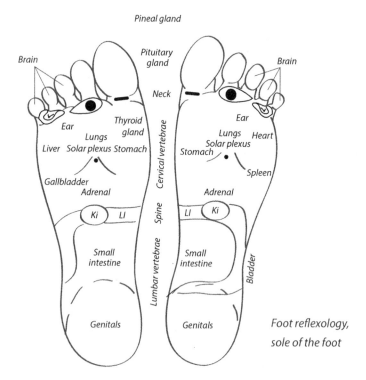

Pineal gland

Pituitary gland

Brain

Neck

Brain

Ear

Thyroid gland

Ear

Lungs

Heart

Lungs

Liver Solar plexus Stomach

Solar plexus

Stomach

Cervical vertebrae

Spleen

Gallbladder

Adrenal

Adrenal

Spine

Ki LI

LI Ki

Small intestine

Lumbar vertebrae

Small intestine

Bladder

Genitals

Genitals

Foot reflexology,
sole of the foot

Then pinch the sides of the toe, start at the insertion of the toe on the foot and slide a bit towards the nail with each next pinch.

Then pull firmly forward on the toe one more time (as if lengthening the toe). You might hear a popping sound in the joint. This is an added benefit to the treatment! After a pop like that you will see that the nail of the toe has become just a bit more pink due to the increase of circulation. More often than not you will not be able to pop the toes. If it doesn't work for you in one or two tries, you can proceed to the next toe and try again during another foot massage.

After you have treated one foot, feel the difference between both feet. Probably the foot that was treated first feels more 'present'. It is also possible that you notice a difference in color between both feet. Many people are amazed that the foot which has been treated is lighter in color than the untreated foot. This difference is color is due to the enhanced circulation in the treated foot.

Treat the other foot the same way.

Different types of massage

The type of massage you use influences the energy differently. Superficial, soft and fast moves make the energy flow faster, which can be clearly felt after the basic massage for the whole body.

Calm, tranquil and deep moves redistribute and start to move stagnated energy. Because this technique may remedy stagnation, the calm – more yin – way of treating has a deeper effect.

Hand massage

Our hands are exceptional body parts. They facilitate everything that we do during the day: from eating and drinking to operating special equipment. Moreover hands tell you a lot about the person they belong to. We shake someone's hand when we meet. That first handshake can reveal all kinds of things about how someone feels. Does someone offer a weak, sweaty hand? A sturdy warm handshake? A cold dry hand? It doesn't matter how self assured you are acting, a clammy hand will give away the fact that you are insecure. On the other hand we can influence our circulation and frame of mind by massaging the hands. Through the meridians this affects worries, sadness, anger, impatience and fear. Was the hand clammy and cold initially? After the hand massage such extreme expressions will have decreased.

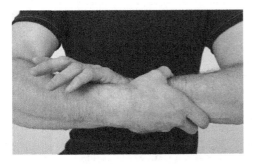

Wrists – Grab the right wrist firmly with the left hand and rotate the right palm back and forth. Through the friction between the left hand and right wrist the joint will be warmed up. It is possible to experience sore spots that have a decreased flow of energy. This massage will improve this.

Palm – Rub your left thumb over the palm of your right hand. Especially rub the cushion at the base of the thumb, which is good for the Lung energy, the center of the palm of the hand, which is good for the Heart energy and circulation. You can also rub along the different lines on your hand. The line near the thumb affects the breath and the digestion, the middle line affects the nervous system and the upper line improves the circulation and the endocrine system.

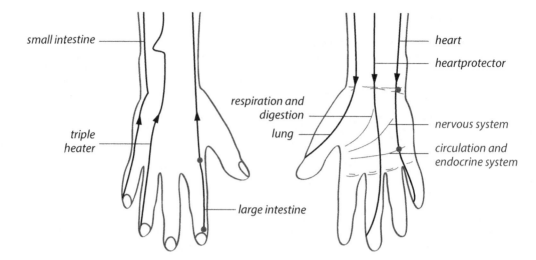

small intestine

triple heater

heart

heartprotector

respiration and digestion

lung

nervous system

circulation and endocrine system

large intestine

Back of hand – Use the fingers of the left hand to rub between the metacarpals of the right hand a few times.

Fingers – grab the thumb and make circular motions with it while keeping the rest of the hand still. Stretch the thumb forwards and backwards as far as it will go. Pinch the sides of the thumb. Starting at the insertion of the thumb to the hand and moving up towards the tip with each pinch. Finally grab the right thumb between the knuckles of the left index and middle finger. Pinch the knuckles together and pull these along the thumbs.
Repeat this on the other fingers.

After you have massaged one hand, take some time to feel. Is there a difference between both hands? Then swap sides.

Lower legs and forearms

The flow of *ki* is easiest to influence between the knees and the toes and between the elbows and the fingers. This is where the yin-meridians (Lung, Spleen, Heart, Kidney, Heart protector, Liver) contact the yang-meridians (Large intestine, Stomach, Small intestine, Bladder, Triple heater, Gallbladder) which they are connected to and vice versa, which makes it easiest to balance a meridian pair. By performing both foot and hand massage, you influence all twelve meridians – and therefore the body in its entirety – in a positive way.

Massage for face and head

Just like with the feet and hands, our head – and more specifically our face – shows exactly how the level of our energy is. Facial diagnosis therefore is also a well know method to therapists who practice Eastern medicine. But you can not only see from the face how you or someone else is doing, you can also influence the flow of energy by massaging your face and head.

Head – Use all ten fingertips of both hands and place them along the hairline above your face. Massage the hairline in a circular motion. Apply light pressure. After a few moments move back about a centimeter (just under half an inch) and keep moving in this way until you reach the edge of the skull on the back of the head. This improves the circulation of the scalp, which offer a sense of relaxation. Daily practice of this technique strengthens the hair and improves hair growth.

Forehead – Use your fingertips to massage your forehead. Start just below the hairline and slowly drop down to the eyebrows. Then rub from left to right a few times and also in reverse over the forehead. Also massage the temples.

Eyebrows – Lightly grab the eyebrows between thumb and index finger, close to the bridge of the nose. Softly pinch or roll them between these two fingers to relieve the tension. Keep moving over bit by bit, so you treat them completely.

Eyes – close your eyes. Use the fingertips of the three middle fingers of each hand to softly apply pressure on the upper edge of the eye socket. You might feel slight indentations in this bone, these are tsubo's. Press your fingers into these indentations three times releasing pressure between each press. Do the same on the lower edge. Subsequently press into the dent on the outer corner of the eye as well as on the edge near the bridge of the nose. You can also apply pressure in circular motions.
Use these same three fingers to apply light pressure between the crease of the eyelid and the bone of the eye socket. Apply pressure here again three times. In the same manner also put pressure on the middle of the eyeball, and then on the crease between the eyeball and the bottom of the eye socket.
Finally use the knuckles of your index fingers to rub under the eyes from the bridge of the nose to the ear, right across the areas where bags appear under the eyes due to fatigue.
These exercises improve the circulation in the eyes, which allows the ability for acute vision to decrease less while we grow old. The skin around the eyes also enjoys better circulation.

This relaxes the small eye muscles and helps to eliminate toxins, which then leads to less formation of wrinkles.

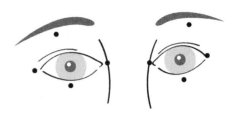

End the eye massage by placing your palms over your eyes (you might want to first rub your hands together a little extra here, so they are nice and warm). Feel how your palms warm your eyes and let the energy from your hands nourish your eyes. Then move the eyeballs, while keeping the eyes closed and covered with your hands, up and down twenty times, and just as many times from left to right and then rotate your eyes in a full circle counter clockwise and next just as many times clockwise.

Nose – Rub along the sides of your nose ten times with your index fingers. Then stick the tips of your index fingers a few millimeter into your nostrils. Pull these away from each other sideways ten times, as well as forwards. After this you can experience that you have more space for breathing through the nostrils and also experience increased flow of energy and draining of mucus. Finally rub back and forth right under the nose ten times.

Mouth, cheeks and jaw – Cross two index fingers along each other while rubbing between the nose and the upper lip. Then press the fingertips under the cheekbones next to the nose. Apply light pressure here for a few seconds on the upper jaw then move the fingers outward towards the mandible joint. Also apply pressure in the same way along the edge of the lower jaw. Rub your palms up and down over the cheeks. And finally rub ten more times over the cheek from the nose towards the ear.

Ears – massage your ear between your thumb and index finger till it gets warm. Pay special attention to the earlobes. According to Eastern medicine the ear shows how strong you are. An ear that has good circulation and is fleshy, as well as with a well defined earlobe, shows a strong constitution.

Fold over the ears a few times.

Place a palm over the ear and knock on this ten times with the other hand.

Stick a finger in the ear and release it with a little jerk, repeat five times.

Finally rub in front of and behind the ear to help drain the toxins more effectively.

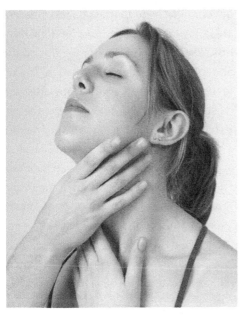

Throat – Stroke from the chin down the neck to the clavicles ten times with flat palms.

These different massages can also be performed on others. You will become a very popular person!

Hara-massage

Our *hara*, the area between the ribcage and the pubic bone, is where our digestion takes place. This area of your body is the source of our daily energy. When the *hara* does not perform properly, we do not extract enough energy from our nutrition to maintain the self healing life force. Massage of the *hara* enhances the circulation in our digestive organs. Besides this the *hara* holds areas which tell us how the twelve major organ meridians in our body are functioning. When you feel a rigid spot on the belly or a very soft one; a very hot area or maybe a very cold one? Then this tells you something about the flow in the meridian connected to it. Performing the *hara*-massage, but also the exercises from part 1, will improve the flow in this meridian.

So whether you want to study which spots represent which organs, or you just want to offer a *hara*-massage following the technique explained below, in both cases it will be truly beneficial to the energy system.

Hara – Lay down in supine position with your feet on the ground, close to your buttocks. Your feet are hip-width apart, and the knees may be relaxed against each other.

If necessary you can rub your hands together to warm them. Use the three middle fingers of your right hand to press on the different areas in your abdomen. Start near the right ribs. Place the fingers under the ribs on the abdomen and softly press them in. The direction of pressure is slanting upwards; you push your fingertips up under the first ribs. You start pushing till you come upon resistance. Register what you come across. Is it hard, soft, warm, cold? If an area is very painful or unpleasant, then retract the fingers calmly. You can warm this area by soft pressure, which helps the tension to disappear. This eases the pain. In other spots you can maintain pressure for one to two minutes; let your hand move along with the motion of the in and exhale. Then move on to the next point. All points along the ribcage can be treated with this diagonal pressure. Also treat all the other areas of the abdomen. The only difference is that you apply the pressure perpendicularly downwards here.

When you find hard area's in the belly, you can apply pressure along the edges of these areas. Repeat this procedure three times a day for the duration of a couple of days. The hard area most likely will have become smaller and more soft.

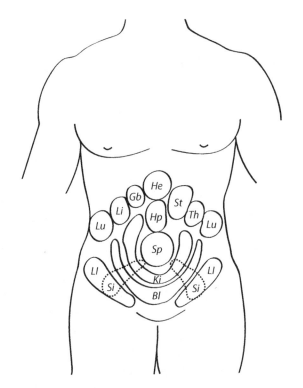

hara massage chart

Lu = Lung
Li = Liver
Gb = Gallbladder
He = Heart
St = Stomach
Th = Triple heater
Hp = Heart protector
Sp = Spleen
Ll = Large intestine
Si = Small intestine
Bl = Bladder
Ki = Kidney

Kyo and *jitsu* in the *hara*

During the *hara*-massage you will probably come across spots that are very soft. These are *kyo* (for theoretical explanation about *kyo* and *jitsu* see Intermezzo 4: powerless or tense: *kyo* and *jitsu*).

The harder or warmer spots are *jitsu*. Sometimes you might find a spot that starts out stiff, but softens quickly when you apply light pressure. This was a hidden *kyo* spot. The body in a sense has built a wall to protect a vulnerable spot which lies beneath. You can strengthen this spot by keeping your fingers there for a longer period, so it warms up nicely.

It is possible to bring more balance between the *kyo* and the *jitsu* areas in the body by applying pressure for longer periods on the *kyo* spots in the *hara*. The spots that are *jitsu* will only be held lightly. This way you can also connect the most *jitsu* area to that which is the most *kyo*. To do this place the fingers of one hand softly on the *jitsu* area and push the fingers of the other hand deeply into the *kyo* area as far as is comfortable. Hold this position until you feel that the *kyo* area fills itself.

2 Breath, the foundation of life

Getting to know your breath

Why a whole chapter dedicated to breathing? Surely we breathe all day already, so you would think we have this technique down quite sufficiently already. Alas not true. Many people that take up Do-In, yoga or Tai Chi for example, do find that they breathe quite superficially, of that they distend their belly on the exhale and pull in the belly on the inhale – in direct opposition to the natural movement of breath.

I hereby invite you to research your breathing. Place your right hand on your lower belly and breathe without influencing the movement. Can you feel a movement in the lower belly? How would you describe this? Now place your left hand just above your belly button and take a minute to sense if there is any movement of breath there. Then place your left hand to your sternum. Can you sense movement there? Is this big, small, fast or slow? Describe these sensations to yourself while getting to know your current breathing. Your breathing tells you a lot about yourself: it is influenced by emotions and activities. When you just wake up, you breathe deep and calm (apart from just shooting awake from a nightmare). When you are in the middle of a rush job, then your breathing is probably superficial and fast. Because your breathing changes often, you can practice this exercise daily to grow closer to yourself.

> **Tip**
> Examine your breath at different times throughout the day. During busy activity, during a moment of relaxation, on the bike or while walking. When you find that you are breathing superficially, place one hand beneath your belly button and one hand above your belly button. Breathe towards your hands.

Healthy breathing

In a healthy, full style of breathing the different areas that you have placed your hand upon (lower belly, diaphragm and chest) move actively along with the breath. That way during each inhalation the lungs fill themselves with a sufficient supply of air to provide the body with oxygen and with each exhalation we release toxins. At the same time this full movement of breath is a massage for our organs. So a 'full' breath means that in each breath the three heaters – the three breathing areas that you have placed your hand upon in the last exercise – move along, it does not mean that the lungs completely fill themselves during each breath.

A healthy style of breathing can prevent or diminish an enormous array of complaints and influences the amount of energy we have. That is the reason why breathing exercises play such an important role during Do-In. Taoists see breathing as the possibility to assimilate *ki* from the air. The air is the true source of life so to speak. Master Kawada, a very devoted shiatsu therapist and teacher from Japan, therefore describes the importance of breath aptly and poetically (Kawada, 2009). He calls it the connection to life and an interplay between heaven and earth, yang and yin. He sees it as an expression of the body to follow the movement of nature and in such a way to live in harmony with it. Taoists time and time again focus their attention on this simple movement, because this helps them to master *ki*.

The breath indeed enables the *ki* to flow. When we breathe our last breath, the flow of *ki* stops and life ends.

If you have noticed that at this particular time your movement of breath is not (always) complete, then the exercises in this chapter are strongly advised, so you can improve your breathing.

Life style

What makes breathing less optimal in so many people? At one time or another surely we were all very good at it. Imagine a sleeping baby, breathing calmly. The breath of a baby is complete. During each inhalation you see the little belly rising, and with each exhalation it moves back down again.

The change in breathing is connected to the modern style of living. Because most people live sedentary lives under quite a lot of pressure, their breathing becomes impaired. Being seated causes tension in the back, chest and abdomen, and at the same time the diaphragm, the flat muscle between the chest and abdomen, is not active enough. This means that the midriff and the lower belly hardly move or don't move along with the breath, and they develop the so called chest breathing. This leads not only to superficial breathing, but also to a diminished flow of *ki*. Apart from this the autonomic nervous system, the parasympathetic system, which calms us, becomes imbalanced.

So breathing better also offers a sense of calmness.

Earlier in this chapter you read that it is important to incorporate all three breathing areas in each breath. There are even more indications of healthy breathing: it runs through the nose and is flowing, silent, deep, calm, relaxed and does not cost any energy. Besides that the transition between the in and exhale flows without jolts or bounces, on average 12-18 times a minute, but slower, for example 6 to 10 times a minute during meditation is normal and considered even more healthy.

Breathing exercises

The following exercises are meant to improve breathing. This also has a positive effect on your state of mind, concentration, digestion, fertility and sexual energy. Apart from that daily breathing and meditation exercises – when you realize that these are an exchange with your surroundings – provide a sense of connection to the rest of the world.

Breathing is always supposed to be as relaxed as possible. The exhale should be longer than the inhale. That symbolizes letting go. This way the exhale provides space for new impressions in the following moment and helps you to connect to the Now.

Breathing into the source

Start out in cross-legged position or in *seiza*. Line up the fingers of one hand on the lower belly right under your belly button. Lightly press the fingers into the belly on the exhalation. Breathe in so deeply that your fingers are pushed out by the breath (and not by the muscle tension!). Repeat this for 5 minutes. If this area is sensitive, you can also place your palm over your lower abdomen and breathe towards your hand.

Even though this exercise sounds simple, for some people it is initially quite difficult. It just seems impossible for them to breathe down into the lower belly. If you also find this is difficult, then don't give up. Repeat this exercise daily for a few weeks, and you will find that it will become more natural for you to breathe deeper. It will probably also provide you with more energy. The fingertips on the lower abdomen after all are stimulating the famous *ki kai* point, which is positioned on the Conception vessel. This point is a powerful source of energy.

Circular breath

Start out once again in a comfortable position. Close your eyes and feel the rhythm of your breath. Imagine that the inhalation runs through your nose over your skull, along your spine through the Governing vessel down to your tailbone (coccyx). On the exhalation you visualize that it flows from the tailbone through the Conception vessel along the bellybutton and breastbone up to your nose. In a sense you imagine your breath to happen in a circular motion in which heavenly (yang) energy flows down and the earthly energy (yin) flows upwards. This stimulates the natural flow of energy in the body and supports an unforced and healthy breathing movement. Repeat this for at least five minutes.

This exercise is done often visualising the flow exactly the other way around: up the back, down the front of our body. If you prefer to follow the energy this way, you could practice this as well.

Cleansing breath

Start out again in a relaxed position with a straight back. Bring your attention to your breath. Imagine inhaling white light with each breath: air full of *ki*. And imagine releasing everything that is no longer useful on each exhalation. You can imagine the things you want to release as grey smoke and exhale them. This exercise provides energy and stimulates the body to eliminate toxins. Repeat for at least five minutes.

Breathing space

Seat yourself in *seiza*, cross-legged position or on a chair. Place your fingertips under your lowest ribs on the abdomen and push them softly inwards under your ribs on an exhale while you bend forwards. This relaxes the diaphragm, offers more breathing space and stimulates the circulation in the organs.

Yin-yang breathing

Start once again sitting upright with a straight back. Bring your attention to your breathing and concentrate for a few minutes.

Fold the index and middle finger of your right hand down towards the cushion at the base of the thumb. Inhale through both nostrils. With the right thumb you close the right nostril and start breathing through the left nostril. At the end of the inhalation you hold your breath for a moment. Open the right nostril and close off the left nostril with the right ring finger. Then breathe out through the right nostril.

Now you inhale on the right. Hold for a few seconds. Close off the right nostril and breathe out on the left. Continue in this fashion and alternate the inhale between the two nostrils. End with an exhale from the right nostril.

This exercise – also known among yogi's under the name of *nadi sudhi* or *anuloma viloma* – has a calming effect, harmonizes yin and yang as well as the left and right side of the body and strengthens the pituitary gland. This is a gland in the brain that regulates the endocrine system.

3 Perspective and stillness
Meditative exercises

Practice without judgment

Many breathing exercises can be used as meditative exercises, periods in which you remove yourself from the stream of thoughts and activities and reside with whatever presents itself in the now. The emphasis here is not on improving your breathing, but on letting things happen as they will and experiencing that which presents itself. Usually you will direct your attention towards an object of meditation, for example the movement of breath in the lower belly. And each time you realize that your thoughts have wandered, you bring your attention back to the object of your meditation.

Those who already know meditation will recognize that thoughts sometimes are more peaceful and at other times present you time and again with little stories. It is of no importance. Recognize this and simply bring your attention back to your breathing. Meditation is not something that you can excel in, it is something that you can revisit time and again, without judgment.

Just like the breathing exercises the meditative exercises are very beneficial. Apart from the relaxation and peace that they offer, they also balance the flow of energies. They move the center of gravity of our attention: from the head to our center, the *hara*. It seems that such a period of relaxation and susceptibility balances the scales which otherwise would have been too heavily burdened with activities and thoughts.

If you don't get carried away with thoughts for a while, you become more grounded, but also more open. That is precisely the reason why during a meditation special realizations may come to you; about yourself, but also about life in general.

Meditative exercises

Seeing the inner light

Begin by sitting relaxed in *seiza*, cross-legged position or on a chair. Close your eyes. Place the thumb and ring finger of the right hand each on one eyelid, exactly in front of the pupil. Only touch this spot, without exerting any pressure. Place your right index- or middlefinger between your eyebrows on the third eye. Concentrate on your breathing.

The fingers on your eyelids prevent the eyes from making any involuntary movements. When your eyes are immobile, it is easier to concentrate. The index finger on the third eye balances yin and yang, opens the sixth chakra (an energy point behind the spot between the eyebrows) and improves deep concentration this way. After a while you might possibly see an inner light. Don't be impatient if this doesn't happen; it will happen another time. Keep focusing your attention on your breathing, especially on the natural break between in and exhalation. Do not get attached to images that appear before your mind's eye or the thoughts that might emerge, but stay focused on your breathing and experience without judgment what you witness.

The first time set aside three minutes for this exercise. Expand this from a half hour up to three quarters of an hour. You can support the elbow of your right arm with your left hand.

This exercise enhances concentration and consciousness, strengthens the flow of energy to the brain, slowly opens the sixth chakra, which enhances intuition. Through this deep concentration you easily connect with the tranquility that is within everyone. Having regular contact with this inner tranquility helps you to experience the world as a supportive pleasant place.

Counting

To reinforce your concentration it can be helpful to count your breaths.

Depart from a meditative position. Count each in and out breath. Count to ten and start over again. You might end up counting to twenty when your thoughts drift. That doesn't matter. Just start over at one and count to ten again.

Just breathing

Start from a calm seated position and follow the movement of the breathing in your lower abdomen. In each inhalation you feel your lower abdomen rise and with each exhalation you feel it fall again. You can attach the words 'rise'...'fall'... within yourself. When you get distracted you name whatever distracted you 'thoughts', or 'memories', and then you bring your concentration back to your breathing again.

Man must be aware not to lose his innate qualities. He must breathe the breath of the universe by controlled in and exhalation
   — Meng Zi (372-289 bC)

Part 3

Do-In programs

Two series to practice on your own

In this chapter the separate elements of Do-In – which were explored in the previous chapters in greater depth – will be combined into a comprehensive program. It is not necessary to have read all of the previous chapters before you start with the two examples of lessons from this chapter. It is fully possible to start with the exercises, and when you feel the need to learn more about the effect they have, you can browse back through the book later.

This chapter offers two programs. One for days when you don't have that much time and one for the days when you have the opportunity to spend more extensive quality time with yourself. The first and shorter sequence includes the so called makko-ho stretches, also known as the Masunaga stretches. These six stretches open the twelve main meridians in a simple yet fast way. This first sequence is also recommended when you suffer from a jet lag. The makko-ho stretches are performed in the order of the Chinese organ clock and therefore harmonise our biorhythm. The second sequence takes more time and offers alternative options to the makko-ho stretches. And of course the exercises from this book can be mixed in endless combinations with each other into new creative programs.

Rules of the game for putting together a program
- Always start off with a breathing or meditative exercise. This helps you to distance yourself from the things you were occupied with, or the things you want to do after Do-In. A moment in the *Now* offers you to experience the Do-In exercises attentively and to experience your body properly so you don't overstep your boundaries.
- Then choose one or more warming-up exercises.
- After this you can alternate between meridian stretches, self-massage and

- breathing exercises. Sequence the meridian stretches according to the Five transformation cycle or the Chinese clock for optimum effect. All meridians should be equally worthy of your attention, even if you want to emphasize a certain meridian with extra stimulation.
- Conclude with a meditative exercise to gather the *ki* in the *hara* and to feel how the exercises have affected you.

1 Short but sweet: Do-In in ten minutes

Introspection

1 minute introspection

Be seated in *seiza*, on your knees with your buttocks on your heels, place your left foot over your right foot, or your left big toe over the right big toe. If this posture is uncomfortable, you can also sit in cross-legged position, on a chair or standing with the feet hip-width apart, toes forward, knees relaxed and pushed out a millimeter, which helps to open the front of the hips. Whichever posture you choose, be sure to lengthen through a straight back. Stack your vertebrae one on top of the other, pull you chin back in slightly towards the chest and push your crown towards the ceiling. Relax your face and shoulders and close your eyes.

Now bring your attention to the movement of breath in your abdomen: feel the inhale and feel the exhale. If you so desire you can place your hands on your lower abdomen to feel this movement more clearly. Breathe at your own pace. When a thought arises, acknowledge it, but do not let it distract you; bring your attention back to your breath. If you are easily distracted, then you can count your breaths. For example you could count three series of five breaths.

Then open your eyes.

Warm up

Basic massage for the whole body

Enhance your circulation and the flow of *ki* in the whole body with this warming self-massage!

Basic position: Stand with your feet hip-width apart. The toes point straight forward and the knees are straight but loose. Now close the hands into a relaxed fist.

Head and neck – start to tap on the head with the relaxed fists. Keep the fists facing each other and travel around your head: the front hairline, the top, the back, the sides and the edge of the skull. Drop down to the neck and tap the side and back of the neck.

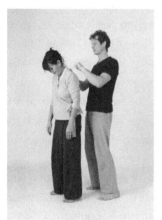

Upper back – Ask someone else to tap on your upper back. This is one area you won't be able to reach yourself! Hang forward slightly while the other person taps all over the back.

Shoulders and arms – Let your right hand tap on the muscles near the left shoulder – skip this step in case of pregnancy. Then run over the pathway of the meridians in the left arm a few times. While doing this you follow the direction of the flow of the meridians. Tap from the shoulder down the inside of the arm to the thumb; this is the Lung meridian. Then return from the index finger on the outside of the arm back to the shoulder; the Large intestine meridian. Subsequently tap the inside of the arm down to the middle finger along the Heart protector meridian. And back up along the triple heart: starting at the ring finger tapping along the midline of the outer arm. Finally tap the inside of the arm to the pinky finger and up along the back outside of the arm; Small intestine meridian. By tapping your arm this way, all of the meridians in this part of the body will experience improved flow.

Also perform the exercise on the other arm.

You can find more information about the meridians in part 1 of this book.

Chest – tap the chest next to the insert of the shoulder joint, just under the clavicle. This is where important acupoints, *tsubo's*, for the lungs are located. Tap the side of the ribcage and then down over the sternum (breastbone). Relaxed chest muscles can literally give you a sense of relief. Moreover this can also help alleviate pain in the upper back, which is often linked to a great deal of tension in the upper thorax.

Abdomen – start near the right hip. Then calmly tap up towards the area just under the right ribs. Tap along the edge of the ribs to the area under the left ribs. Descend down to the left hip. Then travel over to the right hip, creating a number of circles this way over the abdomen. It is important to tap in this direction, because this is the direction that the large intestine flows in. This stimulates the release of toxins.

Lower back and hips – start tapping as high up as you can on your lower back. And then descend to the sacrum and the buttocks, then tap on the hips and the front next to both sides of the pubic bone.

Legs – just like with the arms, we tap on the legs according to the direction of flow of the meridians. The yang- meridians flow down to the toes. The yin-meridians flow up from the toes. Start on the front of the thigh, along the outside of the knee down to the foot; this is the Stomach meridian. Then tap along the inside of the shin and the knee back up to the groin along the Spleen meridian. Subsequently follow the Gallbladder meridian along the outside of the leg down to the top of the foot and come back up along the Liver meridian on the inside of the leg. Finally tap along the Bladder meridian on the back of the leg going down. And follow the Kidney meridian up

again, which is situated right behind the Liver meridian, on the inside back of the leg. This will allow all the meridians in your legs to experience improved flow. More information on the meridians can be found in part 1 of this book.

After this exercise, close your eyes and feel the current sensations in your body.

Bending

This exercise activates the yin-energy bending backwards. The yang-energy is stimulated during the powerful exhalation when you bend forward. The stretches for Conception vessel and Governing vessel empower you, warm you and prepare you for the day ahead.

We now continue from a standing position. Stand up straight. Lift your arms while inhaling, look up and arch the back slightly. Swing the arms to the front, down and back up and forward again while exhaling. At the same time you incorporate bending of the knees in this movement. On the next inhale you raise your arms again. Repeat twenty times and feel the energy flowing through your body after this.

Meridian stretches

The next series of exercises are called 'The six Masunaga stretches' or also 'named 'Makka-ho stretches'. These six postures help to enhance the flow in all meridians.

Tip
If you have the time you can add a meditative quality to this Do-In series by performing the exercises very slowly. Take three to five minutes of time for each meridian stretch. The duration of the opening and closing meditation can be prolonged from ten up to thirty minutes. Be attentive to the difference you will experience between the extra meditative way of performing the exercises as opposed to the version that only takes ten minutes.

Lung and Large intestine stretch in forward bend

Position yourself standing up in medium straddle position. Toes point slightly outward. Hook your thumbs together behind your back. Breathe in and look up, pull your shoulder blades together and open your lungs this way. Exhale and bend forwards from the hips. Stretch your arms up and away from your back and pull your shoulder blades towards each other and slide them down. Sometimes the shoulder blades are stiff and you won't manage to lift the arms away from your back. This is not a problem. Perform the exercise in a way that fits you, this will offer the most optimal effect.

Bring yourself back to an upright position after five to ten full breaths. Hook your thumbs the other way around and perform the whole exercise once again. This exercise stretches open the lungs and the Lung meridians, and also stretches a branch of the Large intestine meridian along the outer back side of the legs.

Beware: In cases of hypertension (high blood pressure) it is not beneficial to hang your head lower than your hips. In this case choose to perform the exercise without the forward bend.

Stretch lying down for Stomach and Spleen

Start positioned on your knees once again, in *seiza*. You can sit on your feet or between your feet. Slowly lean back and walk your hands backwards. Up until here most people can perform the exercise, sitting on a meditation pillow if necessary. Honor your own boundary: lean on your hands or your elbows, or rest upon your shoulders. Push your hips forward to keep your lower back as relaxed as possible. It's okay for your knees to lift off the floor. Once you are lying down on your back, you can bring your hands up over your head and away from you. Place the hands together with the palms facing upwards. Push the knees together as much as you can to stretch the meridians of the Stomach and Spleen simultaneously.

You can lessen the burden of this exercise by placing a pillow or a folded blanket under your back.

Relaxing the upper back for Heart and Small intestine

Sit on your buttocks. Place the soles of your feet together in front of you and pull them in towards you as close as possible. Let your knees fall open. Stretch your back, in such a way that lets you feel your sit bones against the ground. Place your hands around your feet with your left hand over your right hand, without tugging on the toes. Bow your head towards your feet. Your back no longer needs to stay straight, it is allowed to bend. Relax your shoulders and relax your arms. Gravity has enough pull to give you a stretch. Effect: This exercise relaxes your upper back in the region of your heart and the muscles along your shoulder blades, where the pathway of the Small intestine meridian runs, it relaxes the back and enhances the flow in your abdomen. Return to an upright position after five to ten calm breaths.

Forward bend for the Kidneys and Bladder

You begin the exercise sitting on the ground with both legs stretched out in front of you. Pull your toes towards you and let them point upward, so a small stretch is created on the back of your legs. Elongate your back, especially the lower back. Feel yourself resting on your sit bones. If you need to you can bend your legs a little if this helps you to elongate your back. Or sit down on a little pillow. Now bend forward from the hips. Place your hands on the shins, ankles or feet. Stay in this position for five to ten calms breaths. Feel that you still have room for a deep breath, even though the body is folded over.

Shielding

Sit in cross-legged position, with your right leg in front. Move the knees as close to the ground as possible. Breathe in, raise your arms up in a circle, cross the right arm behind the left, bend forward and place the crossed hand upon the knees. Without moving the legs, pull the knees towards each other to open the space in between the vertebrae. Relax the neck. Breathe calmly into the lower belly. After a few breaths return to the upright position. Stretch out while lifting your arms and bring them back down in a circular motion. Now perform this exercise once again in cross-legged position with your left leg in front. This time cross your arms with the left arm behind the right.

Effect: This is a relaxing exercise. The forward bend protects all vulnerable (yin) body parts. The tougher and stronger (yang) parts are now facing outwards. This mirrors the function of the triple heater – which amongst others protects the body from cold – and that of the heart protector – which protects the energy of the heart from intense emotions. The space in between the shoulderblades is connected to the energy of the Heart and Heart protector.

Side stretch for Liver and Gallbladder

The next exercises can also be performed together with a partner as described in chapter 6 about Liver and Gallbladder. Sit down with legs spread wide. Point the toes upward. Straighten your back, elongate your spinal column towards the ceiling and feel your sit bones press against the ground. Now bend sideways with a stretched back, so your flank moves towards the right upper leg. Stretch your left arm over your head and bring your left hand towards your right foot. Body and face remain facing forward, this stretches the flanks and keeps your chest open. Breathe into the ribs on your left side. Come back to upright position after five to ten full breaths and change sides.

Closing

Just breathing

Start from a calm seated position in *seiza*, cross-legged position, or on a chair and follow the movement of the breathing in your lower abdomen. With each inhalation you feel your lower abdomen rise and with each exhalation you feel it fall again. You can attach the words 'rise'…'fall'… within yourself. When you get distracted you name whatever distracted you 'thoughts'… or 'memories'… and then you bring your concentration back to your breathing again.

When you are done, you can give your face a short massage before you open your eyes: rub the palms together until they are warm. This will help to scatter any sleepy sensations after the meditative exercise. Then rub your palms over your face. Finish off by rubbing from your nose towards your ears and down from your ears along the throat. Then open your eyes and calmly stand up from your seated position.

After Do-In

Have a cup of tea or a glass of water after performing Do-In to be able to eliminate the toxins you have released. If you haven't had a lot of exercise for a prolonged period, it is possible you will experience slight dizziness after the first few times you perform Do-In, or even experience a slight headache. This is a sign your body wants to release toxins. In that case drink extra water or tea.

Every so often it is possible that someone experiences fatigue after the first few Do-In lessons. This is almost always a sign that this person has overexerted themselves over the previous period. The Do-In exercises bring you back home to yourself and let you – because they balance the sympathetic and parasympathetic nervous system (your inner accelerator and your inner brake) – experience how you are truly feeling. So it is possible that, after you have turned your focus inwards while performing the exercises, you truly discover how exhausted you are. It is important to listen to this signal from your own body and to allow yourself some extra time to rest and recuperate. Often this clear message your body is sending you turns out to be one of the most precious gifts that Do-In has to offer. After a while you will experience being calm, relaxed and energized after Do-In.

ㄹ Peace and energy: an hour of Do-In

This program is an example of how a Do-In exercise with a teacher could be sequenced. If you perform the exercises calmly, the series will take about an hour. All meridians are offered equally. It is possible to emphasize a specific meridian by adding in more exercises.

Introspection

3 minutes of *seiza* (or any other relaxed position)

Be seated in *seiza*, on your knees with your buttocks on your heels, place your left foot over your right foot, or your left big toe over the right big toe. If this posture is uncomfortable, you can also sit in cross-legged position, on a chair or standing with the feet hip-width apart, toes forward, knees relaxed and pushed out a millimeter, which helps to open the front of the hips. Whichever posture you choose, be sure to lengthen though a straight back. Stack your vertebrae one on top of the other, pull you chin back in slightly towards the chest and push your crown towards the ceiling. Relax your face and shoulders and close your eyes.

Now bring your attention to the movement of breath in your abdomen: feel the inhale and feel the exhale. If you so desire you can place your hands on your lower abdomen to feel this movement more clearly. Breathe at your own pace. When a thought arises, acknowledge it, but do not let it distract you; bring your attention back to your breath. If you are easily distracted, then you can count your breaths. For example you could count three series of five breaths. After this open your eyes.

Warming up

Lifting the knees

From the *seiza* position you lift your knees up one by one, like you are trying to walk on your knees. This exercise stretches the front of the ankles and the insteps, where the Stomach meridian runs. These spots are very rigid in most people. Maybe the first few times sitting in *seiza* on a meditation pillow is already a major challenge. That is a wonderful point of departure. Be kind to yourself and stay within the boundaries of your body. Maybe you will experience that you can remove the pillow after a while, of sit on less of an elevated seat, or that you can lift your knees a small bit. Slowly but surely you will acquire more space.

Stretching the toes

Now lift yourself onto your toes, with your buttocks on your heels to stretch open the sole of your feet. If the stretch is painful, you can adapt by lifting the buttocks a little bit. This alleviates the pressure on your toes.

Effect: This stretch of the toes and sole of the fool enhances the flow of the meridians in the whole body.

Squat

Move back a bit now, so the soles of your feet are flat on the floor. Place your elbows between your knees and fold your palms together. Feel that the back is fully stretched.

If you can't get your feet flat on the floor it might help to widen your stance. If you are still standing on your toes, you can place a rolled up towel under your heels for stability. Is this exercise painful on the knees? Then be seated on the buttocks on the floor with the legs bent and the feet about two feet apart. Place the elbows between the knees in this position.

Effect: This exercise makes the hips more flexible, stretches the yin-meridians in the legs and relaxes the lumbar region.

Back roll

Lay down in supine position. Grab onto the soles of your feet or your knees and softly roll back and forth from the lower back to the area between the shoulder blades. Round out your back as much as possible so all of the vertebrae are massaged against the ground. Feel that the power to roll originates from the hara. Roll back and forth ten to twenty times.

Effect: This exercise stimulates the Governing vessel and the spinal column. This strengthens the back and kidneys, nourishes the brain and bone marrow and clears the mind. Besides that this back roll provides you with energy when you perform it in the morning. And in the evening it ensures that the stagnated energy from your head, neck and shoulders flows further, which helps your mind to calm itself.

Arch

Start out in prone position. Bend your legs and grab your in-steps. If you cannot reach your feet you can hold onto your pant legs, or wrap a shawl around your ankles and hold on to this. Lift up your legs and torso as high as you can on each inhalation to stretch the Conception vessel on the front of your body. Push out the feet upwards and backwards. You can feel the stretch in your chest and abdomen. Relax on each exhale. Try to keep your knees as close together as possible when you lift your legs. Alternative exercise: only lift your shoulders. This exercise as well as the alternative exercise is not suitable during menstruation and pregnancy. Perform it calmly or ask someone to assist you (someone to lift your legs for you) when you are experiencing back problems. After this exercise round out your back as far as you can for a few moments, to counteract this arched posture.

Basic massage for the whole body

Basic position: Stand with your feet hip-width apart. The toes point straight forward and the knees are straight but loose. Now close the hands into a relaxed fist.

Head and neck – start to tap on the head with the relaxed fists. Keep the fists facing each other and travel around your head: the front hairline, the top, the back, the sides and the edge of the skull. Drop down to the neck and tap the side and back of the neck.

Eyes – massage the inner and outer corners of the eye in a circular motion, make five to a hundred small circles.

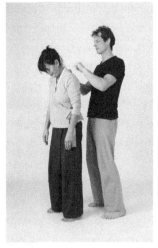

Upper back – ask someone else to tap on your upper back. This is one area you won't be able to reach yourself! Hang forward slightly while the other person taps all over the back.

Shoulders and arms – Let your right hand tap on the muscles near the left shoulder. Then run over the pathway of the meridians in the left arm a few times. While doing this you follow the direction of the flow of the meridians. The yin-meridians run along the inside of the arm towards the finger tips. The yang meridians run along the outside of the arm from the fingertips to the shoulders. Tap from the shoulder down the inside of the arm to the thumb; this is the Lung meridian. Then return from the index finger on the outside of the arm back to the shoulder; the Large intestine meridian. Subsequently tap the inside of the arm down to the middle finger along the Heart protector meridian. And back up along the Triple heater: starting at the ring finger tapping along the midline of the outer arm. Finally tap the inside of the arm down to the pinky finger, Heart meridian, and up along the back outside of the arm; Small intestine meridian. By tapping your arm this way, all of the meridians in this part of the body will experience improved flow.

Also perform the exercise on the other arm.

More information about the meridians can be found in part 1 of this book.

Chest – tap the chest next to the insert of the shoulder joint, just under the clavicle. This is where important acu-points, *tsubo's*, for the Lungs are located. Tap the side of the ribcage and then down over the breastbone. Relaxed chest muscles can literally give you a sense of relief. Moreover this can also help alleviate pain in the upper back, which is often linked to a great deal of tension in the upper thorax.

Abdomen – start near the right hip. Then calmly tap up towards the area just under the right ribs. Tap along the edge of the ribs to the area under the left ribs. Descend down to the left hip. Then travel over to the right hip, creating a number of circles this way over the abdomen. It is important to tap in this direction, because this is the direction that the large intestine flows in. If you suffer from diarrhea, then you can make an exception and tap in the opposite direction.

Lower back and hips – start tapping as high up as you can on your lower back. And then descend to the sacrum and the buttocks, then tap on the hips and the front next to both sides of the pubic bone.

Legs – just like with the arms, we tap on the legs according to the direction of flow of the meridians. The yang-meridians flow down to the toes. The yin-meridians flow up from the toes. Start on the front of the thigh, along the outside of the knee down to the foot; this is the Stomach meridian. Then tap along the inside of the shin and the knee back up to the groin along the Spleen meridian. Subsequently follow the Gallbladder meridian along the outside of the leg down to the top of the foot and come back up along the Liver meridian on the inside of the leg. Finally tap along the Bladder meridian on the back of the leg going down. And follow the Kidney meridian up again, which is situated right behind the Liver meridian, on the inside back of the leg. This will allow all the meridians in your legs to experience improved flow.
More information on the meridians can be found in part 1 of this book.
After this exercise, close your eyes and feel the current sensations in your body.

Meridian Stretches

Opening the Lungs

Stand with your feet a little wider than shoulder width, toes facing slightly outward. Place your hands with fingers interlaced on the back of your skull. Rotate your shoulders down and back. Move your elbows back, open your chest and look slightly upward. Then turn as far as you can to the left. Stand on the toes of your right foot to make the furthest possible turn. Your left foot remains flat on the floor. Push your left elbow up and backwards, so you feel an intense opening stretch in your armpit. Gaze in the distance up along the left elbow. Breath in and out calmly five times. Then turn back to center front and continue through to the right. Perform the exercise on the other side as well. Repeat this two to three times. Effect: This exercise lets you feel a stretch along the pectoral muscles and your upper arm, exactly along the pathway of the Lung meridian. This provides more space for breathing and relaxes your thorax. Lower your arms after you are finished and take the time to feel what the exercise has done for you.

Relaxed neck

From a seated position: bend your left ear towards your left shoulder. You can feel a stretch along the right side of your neck. After five calm breaths you bring your head back to upright position and change sides. Repeat twice more.
Effect: In this position you can feel a stretch along the right side of your neck which follows the pathway of the Large intestine meridian. This relaxes the side of your neck

Balance

Stand up with both feet on the ground. Move your weight into one leg, and pull the other foot to your buttock. Hold the foot with your hand. Keep the knees together. Push your hip forwards and your tail down to relieve pressure in the lower back and keep your upper body upright. To keep your balance it is helpful if you focus your eyes on one spot, but you can also use something for support or lean your free hand against an imaginary wall. Effect: This posture stretches the Stomach and Spleen meridians, this simultaneously relaxes the muscles of the upper legs, which enhances circulation.

When both feet are back on the ground, bring your chin to your chest. Roll down one vertebra at a time, until you are fully bended forward. Then come into a cross-legged position, with your right leg in front.

Linked hands

Now – if possible – fold your right leg even further over your left leg, so your knees are positioned above each other. The insteps of your feet are now resting on the floor. This is sort of an exaggerated cross-legged position. If this position is uncomfortable for your knees, you can stretch out your left leg. Bring your right arm up, bend the arm and place the hand between your shoulder blades. Then bring your left hand behind your back with the elbow bent and you try to link your left and right hand by hooking the fingers together. If this doesn't work, then you can hold a towel or shawl between your hands. After a while you will be able to hold this with your hands closer together, or you might not even need this temporary tool any more. Effect: In this posture you feel the sides of your upper arms stretch open, along the pathway of the Heart and Small intestine meridian; this relaxes the upper arms. In your legs you are giving a light stretch to a branch of the Small intestine meridian. Relax again after five to ten calm breaths.

Forward bend

Now stretch out your legs. Pull your toes towards you and let them point upward, so a small stretch is created along the back of the legs. Elongate your back, especially the lower back. Feel yourself resting on your sit bones. If you need to you can bend your legs a little if this helps you to elongate your back. Or sit down on a little pillow. Now bend forward from the hips. Place your hands on the shins, ankles or feet. Stay in this position for five to ten calms breaths. Feel that you still have room for a deep breath, even though the body is folded over.

Effect: In this posture you feel a stretch of the Bladder and Kidney meridian along the back of your legs and in the back. This stretch enhances circulation in the back as well as your legs because it relaxes the muscles as well as the back. This exercise can offer you peace of mind in periods that are very demanding and also helps to decrease nervousness.

Rubbing

Sit cross-legged or in *seiza* (on bent knees) and place your hands on your lower back – the area of the kidneys. Now start rubbing vigorously over your lower back so that it warms up. After that leave your hands on your back for a minute, so the heat can penetrate inward.

Effect: This exercise is beneficial to the kidneys and relaxes the lower back.

Palms of hands to heaven

Remain seated in *seiza* (on folded knees) or in cross-legged position. Interlace your fingers and push the tips of both the thumbs and pinky fingers together. Stretch your arms up with your palms facing upwards and if possible stretch your elbows – this sounds easier than it is. Relax and let your shoulders drop while you bring your hands up as high as possible, and hold the shoulder blades together on the back; this keeps the muscles between the shoulder as well as the neck relaxed. Make a little roof out of your hands above your head, pulling your wrists slightly apart to achieve this. Breathe in and out calmly five times, and then relax.

Feel your breath all the way down to your lower belly, we often tend to breathe up in our chest when we raise our hands above our head.

Effect: This posture stretches the Heart protector meridian, which relaxes the chest, upper back and inside of our arms.

Back of hands to heaven

After the last exercise reverse the position of your hands so that the backs face upwards. Relax your shoulders while you stretch out your arms as far as you can. You will primarily feel the stretch in the forearms. Bend your body to the left and right to also give the upper arms a mild stretch. Relax after five to ten calm breaths.

Effect: In this posture you are stretching the Triple heater meridian, especially the area near the wrists.

Child's pose with spread knees

Now sit on your knees, with your hips as close to your heals as possible. The insteps are flat on the floor. Open your knees as far as possible, and bend forward with a straight back. Push your sit bones backwards. Place your forehead on the ground and stretch out your arms in front of you. Stay in this position for five to ten calm breaths.

Effect: In this posture you experience a stretch on the inside of your upper legs, exactly along the pathway of the Liver meridian; this opens the hips and enhances the circulation in the legs as well as the sexual energy.

Lubricating the joints

Position yourself on hands and knees. Place the hands directly under your shoulders, your knees directly under your hips. Dig your toes into the ground. Make circular movements with your upper body; your hands and legs remain where they are.

Effect: This exercise lubricates all major joints at the same time (shoulders, hips, knees, wrists and back), so you are supporting the Liver meridian – which keeps the joints flexible – in its task.

Side stretch from cross-legged position

Return to cross-legged position. Place your left hand next to you on the floor. Carry your right arm up past your ear on an inhale and bend over to the left. Keep both of your sit bones on the floor, while stretching your right arm as far away as possible. Breathe in towards the ribs, as if trying to stretch the small muscles between your ribs. Relax your left shoulder down. Stay in this position for five calm breaths, then change sides.

Effect: In this position you will experience a stretch along the ribcage following the pathway of the Gallbladder meridian.

Breathing space

Remain seated in a cross-legged position or move into *seiza*, or sit on a chair. Place your fingertips under your lowest ribs on the abdomen and push them softly inwards under your ribs on an exhale while you bend forwards.

Effect: This relaxes the diaphragm, offers more breathing space and stimulates the circulation in the organs.

Fingers in the lower abdomen

This exercise is also performed from a seated position. Line the fingers of one hand up on the lower abdomen under your belly button. Lightly press the fingers into the belly on the exhalation. Breathe in so deeply that your fingers are pushed out by the breath (and not by the muscle tension). Repeat every day for ten minutes. If this area is sensitive, you can also place your palm over your lower abdomen and breathe towards your hand. Even though this exercise sounds simple, for some people it is initially quite difficult. It just seems impossible for them to breathe down into the lower belly. They simply can't make their breath reach their lower belly. If you also find this difficult, then don't give up. Repeat this exercise daily for a few weeks, and you will find that it will become more natural for you to breathe deeper. It will probably also provide you with more energy.

Effect: The fingertips on the lower abdomen are stimulating the famous *ki kai* point, *Ocean of energy*. This point is a powerful source of energy.

Leg stretch and foot massage

Stretch your legs out in front of you. Place your left hand behind you on the floor.

Grab your right foot with your right hand and stretch out the leg. Calmly swing the leg from left to right ten times. This stretches the Bladder meridian. Now bend the right leg and place the knee in the crook of your right elbow with the foot in the left elbow. You can rock the lower leg in your arms like a baby this way. This opens the Gallbladder meridian near the hips.

Now lower the right leg, so that the ankle is placed on the left upper leg. Grab the right ankle with your right hand. The left hand holds the right foot around the instep. Circle the foot to loosen the ankle.

Sole of the foot – Rub the tips of the thumbs over the sole of the foot from the heel towards the toes, not only over the midline, but also along the sides. Apply light pressure during rubbing. Then tap the fist on the sole of the foot. The tapping technique is the same as that of the *Basic massage for the whole body*.

Instep – Slide over the instep between the metatarsals from the toes toward the ankle. Pay extra attention to the sensitive spots in the groove between the metatarsals. During pregnancy you skip the groove behind the big toe and the second toe. This *tsubo* on the Liver meridian, dissolves stagnation in the energy, which for example alleviates pain, but in rare occasions can induce labor.

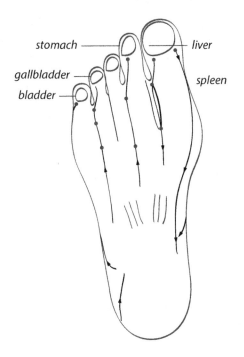

stomach — liver

gallbladder —

spleen

bladder —

Toes – grab your big toe with one hand. With your free hand you can hold on to the ball of your foot to support the joints during the toe massage. While you pull to slightly extend the toe, you make circles with it in both directions. This keeps the joint flexible. After this stretch the toe forwards to the instep as far as possible a few times as well as back down towards the sole of the foot.

Then pinch the sides of the toe, start at the insertion of the toe on the foot and slide a bit towards the nail with each next pinch.

Then pull firmly forward on the toe one more time (as if lengthening the toe). You might hear a popping sound in the joint. This is an added benefit to the treatment! After a pop like that you will see that the nail of the toe has become just a bit more pink due to the increase of circulation. More often than not you will not be able to pop the toes. If it doesn't work for you in one or two tries, you can proceed to the next toe and try again during another foot massage.

After you have treated one foot, feel the difference between both feet. Probably the foot that was treated first feels more 'present'. It is also possible that you notice a difference in color between both feet. Many people are amazed that the foot which has been treated is lighter in color than the untreated foot. This difference is color is due to the enhanced circulation in the treated foot.

Change sides: stretch the left leg and hip first. Then treat the left foot.

Duo arm stretch

This exercise is most effective when performed by two people but is also possible to do by yourself. Stand with your back against that of your partner. Hook your straight arms behind those of your partner, palms facing forward. During an inhalation you both raise your arms so that they are completely stretched upwards. You will experience a stretch along the inside of your arm now, along the pathway of the heart protector. Bring the arms back down on an exhalation and repeat everything three to five times. After completing this, experience the tingling of energy in your hands.

Circular breath

Start out once again in a comfortable position. Close your eyes and feel the rhythm of your breath. Imagine that the inhalation runs through your nose over your skull, along your spine through the Governing vessel down to your tailbone (coccyx). On the exhalation you visualize that it flows from the tailbone through the Conception vessel along the bellybutton and breastbone up to your nose. In a sense you imagine your breath to happen in a circular motion in which heavenly (yang) energy flows down and the earthly energy (yin) flows upwards. This stimulates the natural flow of energy in the body and supports an unforced and healthy breathing movement. Repeat this for at least five minutes. Have this meditation flow naturally into a meditation where you focus your attention on the movement of the breath for at least five minutes.

After this exercise you can take at least five to ten minutes to relax completely. Lay in supine position for this. Place your feet thirty to fifty centimeters (one to two feet) apart and let them fall open. Spread your arms and have your palms facing the ceiling, or place one hand on the area of the heart and one on the lower abdomen.

Bring your attention to your left toes and relax your left leg from the toes to the hip.

Feel the difference between your left leg and your right leg. Then bring your focus to your right leg and relax it from the toes to the hip.

Now bring your attention to your left fingers. Relax the left arm from the fingers to the shoulder. After which you do the same with the right arm.

Then feel the hip area. Relax the whole torso from the hips to the shoulders.

Relax your neck and throat, and follow this with your face: the eyes, mouth, cheeks and the forehead. Relax all of the skin on your scalp.

Enjoy the tranquility and sense of space that you can experience when the whole body is relaxed.

When you sense that you are done, you could – before you open your eyes – give your face a short massage: rub your palms together till they are warm. Then rub your palms over your face. End by rubbing from the nose towards the ears and then finally from the ears down along the throat. Stretch your body out completely from top to toe. Then pull your knees in to your chest and roll from left to right to massage your back. Open your eyes and roll back up over the right side of your body.

In Do-In nothing happens until the moment that you breathe out and thus eliminate toxins.
  — *Jacques de Langre*

In conclusion

After this meditative closure you have completed a voyage through the different disciplines within Do-In hand in hand with this book. You are now capable of combining these in a creative way into your own program, in accordance with the instructions from Intermezzo 5 and 6.

I wish you the greatest of pleasure and an inquisitive mind, so the different exercises – and how they feel – will never cease to amaze you, just as they do for me and many others.

I hope you will enjoy this simple way to strengthen the body over and over again as well as stimulating its self healing properties. And in this way experience that the ancient wisdom of Do-In is still valuable to life in the present.

— Lilian Kluivers

Appendix acu-points

Meridian and number of tsubo	Name of tsubo (Chinese, Japanese, English)	Location	Function
Lung 1	Zhongfu / Chu Fu / Central Treasury	From the nipple 3 thumb widths towards the arm. From there 3 ribs up.	Lung diseases, bronchitis, pain in the chest, asthma, coughing.
Lung 5	Chizé / Shoku Taku / Cubit Marsh	Make a fist and bend the elbow. Lung 5 is located on the thumb side in the crease of the elbow, right next to a muscle (M. Brachioradialis).	Cough, pain in the elbow, painful breathing, sneezing, sore throat, colds, too much saliva, shortness of breath.
Lung 7	Lièque / Retsu Ketsu / Broken Sequence	3 thumb widths from the crease of the wrist on the inside of the arm, on the thumb side. In between the tendon of the M. extensor pollicis and the edge of the radius.	Colds, headache, edema, urinary retention, shoulder problems, heals and harmonizes the flow of energy in the conception vessel.
Lung 9	Tàiyuan / Tai En / Great Abyss	On the crease of the wrist on the inside of the arm, in a small indentation under the cushion at the base of the thumb.	All lung problems, coughing, painful breathing, osteoarthritis in the wrist, turmoil.
Lung 11	Shàoshang / Shou Shu / Lesser Shang	Beside the cuticle on the external side of the thumb.	Sore throat, cough, painful breathing, labored breathing, laryngitis, heart problems, fever, apoplexy (stroke).
Large intestine 1	Shangyáng / Sho Yo / Merchant Yang	At the corner of the cuticle on the thumb side of the index finger.	Pressure on the chest, fever without sweating, toothache, diarrhea.
Large intestine 4	Hégu / Go Koku / Joining of the Valley	In the middle of the web between the thumb and the forefinger. Beware: do not stimulate this during pregnancy!	Diarrhea, facial tension, toothache, problems in the face, nosebleeds, supports the general constitution.

Meridian and number of tsubo	Name of tsubo (Chinese, Japanese, English)	Location	Function
Large intestine 20	Yíngxiang / Gei Ko / Welcome Fragrance	On the lower edge of the nostril in a small indentation.	Stuffy nose, runny nose, facial tension, nosebleeds.
Stomach 3	Jùjiáo / Ko Ryo / Great Bone Hole	When you are looking straight ahead, in a line under the pupils at the level of the bottom of the nose.	Stuffy nose, paralysis of the facial muscles, swelling in the face, night-blindness, myopia, toothaches.
Stomach 25	Tianshu / Ten Su / Celestial Pivot	2 thumb widths next to the belly button, on the edge of the abdominal muscle.	Stomach or Large Intestine problems, pain in the abdomen, diarrhea, rumbling bowel.
Stomach 36	Zúsanli / Ashi San Ri / Leg Three Miles	With knee bent three thumb widths under the lower edge of the patella, one thumb width out (towards pinky toe).	Stimulates the general constitution, provides energy, trouble with digestion, unilateral paralysis, provides support in all cases of chronic diseases.
Spleen 6	Sanyinjiao / San Yin Ko / Three Yin Intersection	Three thumb widths above the largest bulge of the ankle bone (malleolus internus), on the inside of the leg, right behind the tibia. Beware: do not stimulate this during pregnancy!	Insomnia, sore ankles, obesity, digestive problems, irregular menstruation, painful menstruation, trouble with the reproductive system and the genitals.
Spleen 9	Yinlingquan / Yin Ryo Sen / Yin Mound Spring	At the top of the tibia on the inside of the leg, in a small indentation (often painful!).	Knee pain, cold sensation in the lower belly. Pressure point for women to retain their beauty into old age.
Heart 3	Shàohai / Shyo Kai / Lesser Sea	On the bended arm in the corner of the elbow crease on the pinky side of the arm.	Palpitations, ringing of the ears, pain in the elbow, pain in the heart, swelling of the lymph nodes.
Heart 7	Shénmén / Shin Mon / Spirit Gate	In the crease of the wrist on the inside of the arm on the pinky side.	Several diseases of the heart, nervousness, insomnia, point for CPR (reanimation).
Small intestine 3	Hoùxi / Go Kei / Back Stream	When you make a fist, on the pinky side of the hand at the end of the crease under the pinky. Against the side of the metacarpal of the pinky finger.	Sore back, numb sensation in the fingers, pain in the shoulder.

Meridian and number of tsubo	Name of tsubo (Chinese, Japanese, English)	Location	Function
Small intestine 19	Tinggong / Chyu Ku / Auditory Palace	For the ear. With mouth open it is the small indentation that is easily palpable in front of the middle of the ear.	Ringing ears, tinnitus, ear ache.
Bladder 1	Jingmíng / Sei Mei / Bright Eyes	Against the bridge of the nose, just above the inner corner of the eyes.	Poor sight, swollen eyes, blurred eyes, headaches.
Bladder 10	Tianzhù / Ten Chu / Celestial Pillar	On both sides of the long muscle of the neck parallel to the second cervical vertebra, a half centimeter under the edge of the skull.	Headache, hypertension, nervousness, tense neck and shoulders, stuffy nose, pain in the eyes, sleeping disorder.
Bladder 40 (54)	Weizhong / I Chu / Supporting Middle	In the middle of the knee cavity, between the two tendons.	Sciatica, pain in the lower back, tense calves, pain in the knee.
Bladder 60	Kunlún / Kon Ron / Kunlun Mountains	On the horizontal line between the malleolus externus (outer ankle bone) and the Achilles tendon.	Sciatica, dizziness, swollen ankles or knees, challenging delivery.
Bladder 67	Zhìyin / Shi Yin / Reading Yin	Beside the cuticle of the pinky toe, on the outside.	Stimulate with heat (moxa) during breech position in birth.
Kidney 1	Yongquán / Yu Sen / Bubbling Spring	In a cavity in the middle of the sole of the foot. From the insertion of the second and third toe, 1/3 of the length of the foot (minus the toes) towards the heel.	Lack of energy, fear, dizziness.
Kidney 3	Taìxi / Tai Kei / Great Stream	On the horizontal line in between the malleolus internus (inner ankle bone) and the Achilles tendon, you can feel the heartbeat here.	Strengthens the energy of the kidneys, infertility, loss of libido, menstrual disorders, cold feet, exhaustion, insomnia.
Heartprotector 6	Nèiguan / Nai Kan / Yin Cleft	On the inside of the forearm, 2 thumb widths from the crease of the wrist, between the two tendons (of the mm. palmaris longus and the flexor carpi radialis) that run along the length of the forearm.	Nausea, vomiting, insomnia, heart palpitations, fear, pain in the wrist.

Meridian and number of tsubo	Name of tsubo (Chinese, Japanese, English)	Location	Function
Heartprotector 8	Láogong / Ro Kyu / Center of the Palm (Palace of Weariness)	Softly close the fist. Exactly where the tip of the middle finger touches the hand heart protector 8 is located, in the center of the palm of the hand. Apply pressure with the thumb of the other hand.	Exhaustion, painful wrist, stiff fingers, pain in the heart, jaundice, nosebleed, intense emotions.
Triple heater 1	Guanchong / Kan Sho / Passage Hub	Beside the cuticle of the ring finger, on the pinky side.	Nourishes the energy of the heart, the pancreas and the small intestine. Ringing of the ears, vomiting, headache.
Triple heater 5	Wàiguan / Gai Kan / Outer Pass	On the outside of the fore-arm, 2 thumb widths from the middle of the crease of the wrist, between the ulna and the radius.	Rheumatic complaints, hearing problems, flu, headache, pain in the wrist and fingers.
Gall bladder 1	Tóngzijiáo / Do Shi Ryo / Pupil Bone Hole	A half thumb width beside the outer corner of the eye.	Eye problems, headache.
Gall bladder 20	Fengchí / Fu Chi / Wind Pool	In an indentation in the edge of the skull, just behind the insertion of the oblique neck muscle.	Cold, headache, dizziness, swollen eyes, pain and stiffness in the neck and shoulders.
Gall bladder 21	Jianjing / Ken Sei / Shoulder Well	At the highest point of the shoulder. Beware: do not stimulate this during pregnancy!	Headache, neck and shoulder pain and stiffness, head full of thoughts.
Liver 1	Dàdun / Dai Ton / Big Mound	Beside the cuticle of the big toe, on the side of the second toe.	Cramp, headache, menstrual problems, pain in the genitals.
Liver 3	Tàichong / Tai Chu / Great Surge	One thumb width from the joints between the big toe and the second toe, between the metatarsals. Beware: do not stimulate this during pregnancy!	Stimulates the energy of the liver, trouble with the liver, pain in the foot, pain in the stomach area, muscle spasms, headache, wetting the bed, cramp, insomnia.
Gouverneursvat 16	Fengfu / Fu Fu / Wind Mansion	In the center of the edge of the skull in an indentation.	Headache, nosebleed, cold, flu, dizziness.

Meridian and number of tsubo	Name of tsubo (Chinese, Japanese, English)	Location	Function
Gouverneursvat 20	Baihùi / Hya Kue / Hundred Convergences	On the middle of the top of the skull, draw a line between the two highest points of the ears.	Headache, forgetfulness, hemorrhoids, nervousness, hypertension, cold, hernia, constipation.
Conception vessel 4	Guanyuán / Kan Gen / First Gate	Two thumb widths above the pubic bone, straight under the bellybutton.	Provides energy for the small intestine, mental fatigue, intestinal problems, prolongs life, impotence, lower abdominal cramps also during menstruation, fears.
Conception vessel 6	Qìhai / Ki Kai / Sea of Ki	1,5 Thumb widths under the belly button.	General weak constitution, infertility, having trouble conceiving, kidney and bladder problems, stomach ache, diarrhea, menstrual pains, wet dreams, constipation, represents the second chakra - the physical center.
Conception vessel 12	Zhongwan / Chu Kan / Central Venter	Between the belly button and the sternum (breastbone).	Nausea, diarrhea, vomiting, stomach problems, diabetes, represents the third chakra, the centre of ego identity.
Conception vessel 17	Tánzhong / Dan Cha / Chest Center (Sea of Tranquility)	On the breastbone, on the level of the nipples, often feels like a bruise.	Asthma, hypertension, shortage of milk during breastfeeding, pain in the heart or the chest, pain in the breasts, depression, nervousness, vomiting, represents the heart chakra, (self) treatment of this point dissolves emotional bruises.

Acknowledgements

Many thanks to all of the people who have contributed to the realization of this book. I especially thank dr. Y. sensei Kawada, who is one of my greatest sources of inspiration. My shiatsu and Do-In teachers, Alan Nash and Anushka Hofman, with whom I had a great time working at her education. And thanks to Cathy de Geest, Do-In teacher and shiatsu therapist, who focused her keen scrutiny on the different chapters, I owe her my gratitude. Besides that I am grateful for my good friend Alette Bakkers. She has provided criticism for the different chapters from the point of view of a beginners mind, which enormously helped me to explain the sometimes complex subject matter in a clear way.

Thanks to Imgriet Luppe, for your supportive wisdom. I also thank all my students at the Do-In Academy and other educations I have taught for, and the people that have joined my workshops and weekly classes, because they also provide me with renewed inspiration time and again.

This book was first published in the Netherlands. Many thanks to Reinoud Douwes and Gerolf t Hooft, for the trust you have put in me by asking me to write this book for you, and Natacha Weber for helping me with the finishing touches. Thank you Dorine Esser, for drawing these gentlemen's attention to the possibilities of this book. Thank you Yoff Kau, for taking the time and effort to translate this book.

And finally I thank my sweet life partner Bas and dear daughter Niya, who are always there for me.

About the author

Lilian Kluivers is head of Do-In Academy, an international education for Do-In. She teaches Do-In classes, workshops and does personal consultations in which she integrates the oriental wisdom of Do-In, shiatsu, nutrition, astrology and lifestyle. Lilian integrates her knowledge and experience and let it come to life through Do-In. She can connect East and West so we can all benefit from the wisdom and practice in our daily life.

She has taught at several teachers training institutes and has internationally published press-articles on the subject of Do-In. Most can be found on her own websites.

Her second book is focussed on pregnancy. Pregnant women and their partners learn how to work with Do-In during pregnancy and birthing, for an optimal energy flow for the mother and child.

www.doinacademy.com
www.liliankluivers.nl
YouTube channel: Do-In Academy

Recommended literature

Books on the subject of Do-In

Kushi, Michio, *The Do-In Way, Gentle Exercises to Liberate the Body, Mind, and Spirit*. New York: Square One Publishers, 2007 (Also published under the title *The book of Do-In*; New York: Japan Publications, 1979)

Langre, Jacques de, *Second Book of Do-In, Art of Rejuvenation through Self-Massage*. Magalia: Happiness Press, 1974

Masunaga, Shizuto, *Meridian Exercises; The Oriental way to health and vitality*. Tokyo/New York, Japan Publications Inc, 1996

Rofidahl, Jean, *L'art du Do-In: Se renouveler chaque jour*, Lausanne, Editions du Signal, 1978

Related literature

Beresford-Cooke, Carola, *Shiatsu theory and practice; Dutch translation*. Churchill Livingstone, 1995

Chia, Mantak, *Energy Balance through the Tao; Excercises for Cultivating Yin Energy*. Vermont: Destiny Books, 2005

Chia, Mantak, *Chi Self-Massage, The Taoist Way of Rejuvenation*. Vermont: Destiny Books, 2006

Cooley, Bob, *The Genius of Flexibility; The Smart Way to Stretch and Strengthen your Body*. New York: Fireside, 2005

Dürckheim, Karlfried Graf von, *Hara: The Vital Center of Man*, Inner Traditions. 2004

Gach, Michael Reed and Marco, Carolyn, *Acu-yoga; designed to releave stress and tension*, Tokyo, Japan Publications, 1981

Gach, Michael Reed, *Acupressure; How to Cure Common Ailments the Natural Way*. Bath: Piatkus, 1991

Kaptchuk, Ted J., *The web that has no weaver*. Contemporary books, 2000

Kawada, Yuichi and Karcher, Stephen, *Essential Shiatsu; Essential Shiatsu for Troubled Times*. London: Piatkus, 2009

Lundberg, Paul, *The Book of Shiatsu: A Complete Guide to Using Hand Pressure and Gentle Manipulation to Improve Your Health, Vitality and Stamina*, London, Gaia Books Ltd. 1992

Maciocia, Giovanni, *The Foundations of Chinese Medicine; A Comprehensive Text for Acupuncturists and Herbalists*. Oxford: Elsevier Ltd. 2006

Masunaga, Shizuto and Ohashi, Wataru, *Zen-Shiatsu; How to Harmonize Yin and Yang for Better Health*, Tokyo, Japan Publications, 1977

Namikoshi, Toru, *Touch and Stretch: shiatsu for everyoneI*, Tokyo, Japan Publications, 1985

Ni, Maoshing, *The Yellow Emperors Classic of Medicine; A New Translation of the Neijing Suwen with Commentary*. Boston: Shambhala, 1995

Ohashi, Wataru, *Do-It-Yourself Shiatsu; How to Perform the Ancient Japanese Art of 'Acupuncture without Needles'*. New York: Penguin Books, 1992

Ohashi, Wataru, *Reading the body, Ohashi's book of oriental diagnosis*, New York, Arkana Books, 1991

Temelie, Barbara, *The Five-Elements Wellness Plan: A Chinese System for Perfect Health*, Sterling, 2002

Temelie, Barbara and Trebuth, Beatrice, *Die praktische Umsetzung der chinesischen Ernährungslehre für die westliche Küche – 200 Rezepte zur Stärkung von Körper und Geist*, Taschenbuch, 2002

Yamaoka, Seigen, *The Art and Way of Hara*, Heian international, 1992

Yates, Suzanne and Anderson, Tricia, *Shiatsu for midwives*. Eastbourne: Elsevier Science Limited, 2003

Glossary of terms

Chi of Qi: the Chinese word for *ki* which is best translated with life force energy.

Essence: the most basic energy from which the yin and yang energies are formed

Hara: Abdomen, the center of your body and in that capacity very important in Eastern medicine.

Jitsu: to be interpreted as "full". Eastern medicine uses this term to indicate that a certain part of the body or side of the body is more stiff or rigid than the other side. The more relaxed side is referred to as *kyo*. Performing the postures with the flexible side first stimulates the body to redistribute the energy equally over the body.

Ki: the Japanese word which is best represented by the concept of life force energy (Chinese translation is *Chi*).

Ki Kai: the energetic pressure point located three widths of a finger under the belly button. The meaning of the name of this point is 'ocean of energy'.

Kyo: to be interpreted as 'empty'. Eastern medicine uses this term to indicate that a certain part of the body or one side of it is more flexible, but also less powerful, than the other side. The more tense side is called *jitsu*. Performing the postures with the flexible side first stimulates the body to redistribute the energy equally over the body.

Makko-ho: the six exercises which were presented as a consecutive series by the Japanese shiatsu therapist and psychologist Shizuto Masunaga, are called the Makko-Ho exercises, after the man who first combined five of these exercises.

Mudra: body posture (often of the hands) which influences the energy.

Postnatal energy: the energy that we produce after our birth by means of breathing and nutrition.

Prana: the Indian word which is best represented by the concept of life force energy.

Prenatal energy: the energy that we receive from our parents. Also referred to as *yuan-ki*.

Ren mai: Chinese name for the Conception vessel, one of the so called extraordinary (curious) meridians, which together with 7 other extraordinary meridians (including Du mai) in summary act as a back-up for the 12 normal meridians.

Shen (Shin): The seat (soul) of the heart, our consciousness.

Tan Den/Tan'Tien: powerful energetic points on the crown, between the eyebrows, under the sternum and three finger widths under the belly button. The latter is used most within Do-In.

Tsubo: The Japanese word for pressure point

Register

Made in United States
North Haven, CT
27 February 2023